W9-AAF-076

"A truly charming book, and I very much enjoyed reading through it."
Michael Korda, Corporate Vice President, Editor-in-Chief
Simon & Schuster

"A Family Love Letter . . . this cookbook is like a long love letter to one's family — a paean of hearth, heritage, and home. Like the best kind of letter, **Grandmother's Cookbook** *is written by hand from the heart. It has flower pressed between its pages as a true love letter should — and like all love letters, it will be taken out and read over and over again."*
Lisa Kingsley, Food and Garden Editor
Country Home Magazine

"Elizabeth von Hohen & her granddaughter have preserved a piece of the past with **Grandmother's Cookbook.**"
Lady's Circle Magazine

"Charming is a modest word to use for this tastefully produced cookbook."
The Book Reader

"A treasure of remembered tastes and a beautiful tribute to the special relationship that can exist between a grandmother and her grandchild."
The Monterey County Herald

"Elizabeth Rose von Hohen kneaded and cut thousands of Hungarian noodles over the decades following a recipe that existed in her mind's eye and in her practiced hands . . ."
The Associated Press

'The lovely flowers and the little notes make it a storybook. I am absolutely enchanted by it! If one never used a recipe they could have hours of pleasure just reading it!"
Mildred Field, Cookbook Collector

"An absolute delight! You have created a real keepsake. For your effort, labor, creativity and love that went into this book, I thank you!"
Sharon Opsal, Cookbook Collector

Wisteria

Our wisteria was a grand thing! My brothers built an arbor over the driveway for the vine to grow on. It took awhile to get started, but then grew as if possessed. In the spring it was something to behold. The big clusters of purple flowers looked like bunches of grapes and were so fragrant! They were always full of bees too. In fact, we had a beehive in our attic because of the wisteria. I remember our neighbor helped us take it down one day and we got a wash tub full of fragrant honey from it!

(shown on title page)

Preface

When my grandmother and I decided to write this book several years ago the idea was to have all of her special recipes written down so they would not be lost forever. I feel fortunate to have them. Through the thousands of letters we have received we've learned many people have not been so lucky. Their "lost recipes" seem to be found in one way or another with our book.

We have also discovered there is something more than recipes which many have found within these pages. For renowned chef Bradley M. Ogden our book recalls treasured memories of times spent at his grandmother's farm. For Barbara Davis Taylor, Food Writer for The Monterey County Herald, it stirs memories of sipping tea and capturing recipes from her grandmother. A 93 year old woman reminisces over "fond memories of the smell and goodies which came out of my own grandmother's kitchen with only a coal-wood stove that produced never-again tasty foods which I enjoyed so much as a very young girl." For a trans-planted American living in Saudi Arabia this book helps to fill a gap for the mother she lost at an early age, the grandmothers she never knew and her lost family recipes.

I am happy to be able to share my grandmother's delicious recipes and equally as happy that this book recalls such wonderful and vivid memories of a time when life was simple and family traditions were still going strong. This all seems to be summed up in a light-hearted note we recently received – "Thanking you in advance for many enjoyed meals that call up memories of yesterdays."

Carrie J. Gamble

Foreword

My children and grandchildren have been after me for years to write down all of those special things I learned to cook from my mother. She came to America from Austria-Hungary and raised us on the food they ate over there. We never had much meat, once or twice a week and of course on Sunday. Otherwise we ate things made from dough. Dumplings and noodles as well as potatoes and vegetables in season. All these foods were prepared in special different ways so were never monotonous. Mother could bake wonderful bread and all kinds of goodies made from yeast dough. Her cookies were delicious! They were made with real home-made butter and faintly flavored with lemon peel, nutmeg or cinnamon. We had no other flavorings. They were always moons or half moons cut out with a glass as we had no cookie cutters.

When I finally went to school I would come home and tell my mother of all the wonderful things my girlfriends brought in their lunches. From this we got new ideas. I would read her the recipes (I was about nine at the time) and together we would try new things. I'll never forget our first pie - Butterscotch. We were so pleased with ourselves! And when she made her first layer cake! It was for my last day of school. In our little country school the last day was always a picnic and everyone brought a goodie. Mother had no layer tins so she made it in a big bread pan. She sliced it in half to make two layers. Then she iced it. I was so proud of her! I think I stopped every ten minutes on my way to school to admire it!

Needless to say, all of this fostered a great love of cooking in me. I am always ready to try new things.

I also had a Bohemian godmother, my Aunt Rose. She had been a cook in Vienna for an aristocratic family. She could make wonderful pastries and cakes. We were very close and she shared many very special things with me including her cooking experience.

When I was sixteen I went to Philadelphia and got a job as a cook with a wealthy Jewish family. I gained much experience there.

It was my boss, Mrs. Strauss, who taught me many recipes which through the years have been among my family's favorites.

So now I am an old lady whose family is all grown up. But I still love to cook and try new things. To be really good at anything you have to love it.

I hope these recipes turn out well for anyone who uses them. Although I've tried to be very explicit in my writing, you will have to keep in mind that some of these recipes take practice. You have to learn the right texture and feel and taste of things, so it's up to the cook. In writing this book my hope is that all these special old fashioned recipes will not become a lost art.

Elizabeth Rose von Hohen

In 1934, in the fields
of the family homestead,
Elizabeth holds her
beloved wildflowers

Table of Contents
Soups

Breads

Dumplings and Noodles

Appetizers and Salads

Meats and Vegetables

Desserts

Christmas Specialties

The Staff of Life

When I was a little girl growing up on the farm my father always said, "Bread is the staff of life. As long as you have bread you won't go hungry." We had homemade bread with every meal and in old country tradition, my mother baked her own. She baked 8 large loaves a week. We'd cut off a thick slice by holding it in one arm and cutting with the other, just like the "Ceresota boy" on the brand of natural unbleached flour our family has been using for four generations. My mother swore by this flour as it made wonderful bread and kept well all week.

During the First World War unbleached flour was rationed. My mother had to use what was available and got very frustrated as her bread lacked its usual fine texture and did not keep.

My granddaugther called Ceresota and Heckers brand flour company to find out why it is better. With interest she learned that it was specifically developed for the immigrants from mid and northern Europe. It is made from hard winter wheat, is high in protein and therefore better for baking. Most of my recipes call for flour. Choose your brand carefully. It <u>does</u> make a difference!

Soups

Wild Roses

    Did you ever walk down a country lane in the summertime and see the wild roses blooming in the fence row? I've always loved their delicate rosy pink blossoms and spicy fragrance. Once you have seen them, you will never forget.

Vegetable Soup with Dumplings

Use a nice piece of shin meat with a marrow bone in it. Put the meat into a 4 qt. pot. Fill with water and cook until boiling. Turn down to simmer. Add all of the diced vegetables. I use everything, 2 carrots, a piece of turnip, 2 stalks celery, 1 large fresh tomato or ½ cup stewed tomatoes, 1 onion, 1 clove garlic, 1 bay leaf, 3 cloves, a few slices of cabbage leaves, some green pepper, a package of mixed frozen vegetables, 1 tablespoon salt and a dash of pepper. I also like to add 2 tablespoons barley or rice, whichever you prefer. Let it all simmer together for at least 2 - 3 hours. When it's done, add the dumplings.

For the dumplings: In a bowl mix 1 cup flour, a pinch of salt, 1 egg and enough water to make a stiff dough. Take a teaspoon and cut off ½ teaspoon size of dough and drop into the soup. Cook about 5 minutes until they rise and are done. Cut the meat into bite sized pieces and put back into the soup. Sprinkle a little chopped parsley on top before serving. This soup is a meal in itself.

Tomato Soup with Egg Drop

Put a good tablespoon of margarine into a pan. When melted add a heaping tablespoon of flour. Blend well and brown slightly. Take 1 qt. fresh or canned strained tomatoes. To the margarine and flour mixture add the tomato juice and a cup of water. Bring to a boil. Add a bay leaf, salt, pepper and a little sugar to taste. Cook for about 5 minutes.

For the egg drop: Take a ½ cup of flour, pinch of salt, one egg and enough water so it will pour from a cup. Then, while the soup is boiling, drizzle it back and forth into the soup. Stir once or twice with a fork while drizzling. Cook 2 minutes. Before serving you can slowly add a cup of milk. This gives it a creamy texture and flavor.

A pinch of baking soda added makes it less tart and the milk will not curdle.

Potato Soup sweet potatoes
3-28-2022

For this soup it's nice to have leeks. If not, use scallions or <u>onions</u>. Put 2 tablespoons <u>of margarine</u> in a pot. When melted add ½-3/4 cup minced leeks, scallions or <u>onion</u>. Let it cook to golden brown. Add 1 tablespoon <u>flour</u>. Mix well. Add <u>4 cups water</u> and 1 <u>chicken bouillon cube</u>. Peel and dice 2 large potatoes and add them to the broth. Add a teaspoon salt and a dash pepper. Cook about 20 minutes until the potatoes are done. Then <u>I mash them with a fork</u>. Add <u>1 cup milk,</u> a pinch of mace and 1 tablespoon of chopped ✱ <u>parsley</u>. Bring to a boil. Cook for 5-10 minutes until the soup gets slightly thick. Take off →heat. Sprinkle each serving with parsley. Serve with crackers.

∽

With potato soup or vegetable soup we usually make a meal of it. Then we have a good dessert, like cinnamon buns, apple cakes or strawberry shortcake. A favorite dinner with all of us.

German Meatball Potato Soup

Peel 2 potatoes and cut into small cubes. Take 3 slices bacon, cut into small pieces and fry until light brown. Then add 1 finely chopped onion, one large leek and steam lightly. Do not brown. Add 1 qt. water and 2 chicken bouillon cubes. Then add potatoes, salt, pepper and thyme to taste. Cook about 3/4 of an hour.

To make the meatballs: Use 1/2 pound ground meat mixed with 1/4 cup bread crumbs, 1/4 teaspoon salt, pepper, 1 small chopped onion, 1 egg and a pinch nutmeg. Mix well. Roll in your hands and make small balls, the size of large marbles. Drop into the boiling soup. Add 1/2 cup stewed tomatoes. Cook about 10 minutes. Add a sprinkle of chopped parsley and serve. A great one dish meal. Can be prepared ahead of time.

Sausage Bean Chowder

Take one pound of pork sausage. Brown in a dutch oven stirring to separate the meat. Add 2 cups water, 1-16 oz. can kidney beans, 1-16 oz. can stewed tomatoes, 1 finely chopped onion, 1 large potato (peeled and cubed), 1/4 cup chopped green pepper, 1 bay leaf, 1/4 teaspoon salt, pinch of thyme, 1/4 teaspoon garlic powder and 1/4 teaspoon pepper. Cook until vegetables are done. This usually takes about 1/2 to 3/4 of an hour. Serve with crackers.

This is another good one dish meal which can be made ahead of time.

Bean Soup

Cook 2 cups of navy beans for about 5 minutes. Drain. Put into a 4 qt. pot. Add a nice ham bone or ham broth. You can also use smoked sausage if you don't have the ham. Add about 3 qts. of water and boil. When it starts to boil add all kinds of vegetables. You can use frozen mixed vegetables, but I like to use fresh. 1 cup sliced cabbage, and the following diced vegetables: 1 onion, ½ cup turnip, ½ cup celery, 1 tomato, piece of pepper, peas and string beans. Add 1 clove garlic, 2 cloves, 1 bay leaf, 1 sprig of thyme, 2 tablespoons barley. Salt and pepper to taste. Simmer for at least 2 hours until beans are soft and done. This gets nice and thick. We like to add a few dumplings too.

For the dumplings: take 3/4 cup flour, pinch salt, 1 egg and enough water to make a stiff dough. You can cut ⅛ teaspoon pieces and drop into boiling soup. When they rise to the top, they are done and the soup is ready.

Split Pea Soup

Very good

1 pound split peas, ham broth or ham bone, 1 onion, clove garlic, 3 cloves, 1 stalk celery, 2 carrots, sprig thyme or dried thyme, salt and pepper to taste.

Wash peas. Put them in a pot with 3 quarts of water and the vegetables and seasonings. Simmer for about 2 hours until peas are soft. Strain through a sieve. Push peas and vegetables through with a wooden spoon to make a nice creamy consistency. Discard what remains in sieve. Put creamy broth back into the pot. Salt and pepper to taste. Add thinly slices knockwurst or diced fried bacon. Bring to a boil. Then it is ready to serve. I usually sprinkle each serving with croutons.

Katie & Lily,
Grandma's & great grandma's
fav soup!
I love you.

Ham bone from
Anniversary!
BUG

Chicken Noodle Soup

Take a small chicken (about 3 pounds) or just use breasts and put it on with about 3 quarts water. Add 2 carrots, 1 onion, 1 clove garlic, 1 stalk celery, sprig of thyme and parsley, 2 cloves, salt and pepper. Bring to a boil and simmer for about 1-1½ hours or until chicken is done. Remove chicken. Strain broth. Save the carrots and discard everything else. Slice carrots. Bring broth to a boil. Add fine home-made noodles or now one can buy them. Add ½ of the sliced carrots and save the other ½ for the creamed chicken. When noodles are tender sprinkle with chopped fresh parsley and serve.

Creamed Chicken

Take all of the meat from the soup and cut into pieces. Discard all of the bones. Slice up carrots from soup. Cook ½ cup peas. Melt 2 tablespoons margarine and stir in 2 tablespoons flour. Cook until smooth, a few minutes. Add 1 cup ea. of chicken broth and milk. Cook until smooth. Add more broth if too thick. Add chicken pieces, carrots, peas, salt and pepper to taste. Serve on buttered toast points.

Creamed Vegetable Soups

For asparagus, broccoli, cauliflower, cabbage and spinach soups.

This is a good way to use leftover vegetables or you can cook them fresh. I always reserve a cup or so of the water the vegetables were cooked in. This really adds to the flavor of the soup. Melt 1 tablespoon butter or margarine. Add a heaping tablespoon flour and stir until well blended. Add your vegetable broth with a cup of chicken stock made with 1 cup of boiling water and 1 bouillon cube. Let this come to a boil then add a generous cup of the chopped vegetable. Add a cup of milk. Stir until smooth. Salt and pepper to taste. If too thick add some more water. Serve with crackers or croutons.

For asparagus, broccoli and cauliflower add ⅛ teaspoon mace. This makes a very special flavor.

One can always sprinkle on some grated cheese if preferred, or you can add a ½ cup or so in with the soup for extra flavor.

11

Corn Chowder

6 slices of bacon, 1 medium onion finely chopped, 2 medium potatoes peeled and cubed, 1 cup water, 1 small can of stewed tomatoes, 2-3 ears of fresh corn or 1 package of frozen corn, 1/2 teaspoon salt, dash pepper, 1 bay leaf, 1 teaspoon sugar, 1 cup milk and 1/2 tablespoon flour.

Fry bacon in dutch oven until crisp. Remove bacon and set aside. Leave 2 tablespoons of the drippings in the pan and saute onions in that. Add 1/2 tablespoon flour and mix in with onions. Add potatoes and water and cook until potatoes are soft. This takes about 20 minutes. Add tomatoes and corn and cook about 5 minutes. Add 1 cup milk and spices. Cook until well heated. Serve with crumbled bacon sprinkled on top. This yields about 5 cups.

Breads

Trailing Arbutus ♡

    I'll never forget Dora. She was my friend at school when I was a little girl. Every spring Dora would come in with a little bunch of fragrant pink flowers pinned to her dress. I just loved them. She told me they were trailing arbutus and grew in the woods. I always wanted to see them growing wild, but could never find any.

    Many years later for my birthday, my granddaughter called a nature center in New Hope. She asked if they knew where we could see the trailing arbutus grow. The nice man told her of a local church where they grow wild in the cemetery. So for my 19th birthday on a warm April afternoon she took me there. There they were, growing and spinning over the mossy ground like little white and pink stars with small round green and bronze leaves. All scattered throughout the old cemetery with it's weathered, broken tombstones beside this little old country church deep in the woods. I was so happy to finally see trailing arbutus grow! It was one of my nicest birthdays and I will never forget it.

Feather Beds

"Aunt" Cheryl

1/3 cup sugar
1 teaspoon salt
1/4 cup margarine
3/4 cup hot potato water
1 package yeast
1/2 cup warm mashed potatoes
1 egg
4 - 4 1/2 cups flour

Stir together sugar, salt, mashed potato water and margarine. Let cool. Add the rest of the ingredients and knead well. Let rise until double in bulk. Then roll out and cut into circles. Put close together on a baking sheet. Let rise again until double. Bake at 350 degrees for 30 minutes until golden.

These may also be made into crescent rolls and clover rolls. They are very light and most delicious.

Oatmeal Bannock

2½ to 3 cups flour
⅓ cup sugar
3/4 teaspoon salt
1 cup uncooked oats
2 packages yeast
½ cup milk
½ cup water
¼ cup margarine
1 egg
1 cup currants

Mix 3/4 cup flour, the oats, sugar, salt and yeast in a bowl. Combine milk, water and margarine in a saucepan and warm on a low heat on the stove. Add to flour mixture and beat 2 minutes. Add the egg and the rest of the flour and knead until smooth. Let rise until double in bulk. Punch down. Add currants and knead until they are evenly distributed. Divide the dough in half. Form each half into an 8" circle. With a knife mark 8 wedges on top of the dough. Let rise until double in bulk. Bake at 350 degrees for 20 minutes or until golden brown. Delicious with lamb stew.

Sesame Twist Bread

Warm 1¼ cups milk. Add 3 tablespoons honey, 2 tablespoons shortening, 1 teaspoon salt and 1 egg. Dissolve 1 package yeast in ¼ cup warm water. Stir all ingredients together and add 4 cups of flour. Mix well. Knead until smooth. Put in a warm place in a covered bowl and let rise until double. Then take out and knead again. Cut dough into 3 pieces. Roll each into a rope about 14" long. Pinch together at one end and braid together into a loaf. Pinch the other end together. Let stand and rise again. When doubled, brush with egg yolk mixed with a little milk. Sprinkle with sesame seeds. Place in a well greased pan. Bake at 375 degrees for 45 minutes.

You can add an extra egg and a pinch of saffron for a richer bread.

Crusty French Bread

6 cups sifted flour
2 tablespoons sugar
1½ teaspoons salt
2 tablespoons vegetable shortening
1 package yeast
2 cups very warm water

Dissolve yeast in very warm water. Stir in 3 cups flour and the sugar, salt and shortening. Beat until real smooth. Slowly add the rest of the flour. Knead until smooth. Put into a greased bowl, cover and let rise until double. Punch down and let rise again. Put the dough on the table and knead. Cut into 2 pieces. Roll out each piece into a 9"x 12" rectangle. Then roll each up like a jelly roll, tucking the ends under. Grease cookie sheet and sprinkle with corn meal. Place the loaves on it. Slash top of loaves crosswise ½" deep and 2" apart. Let rise until double. Brush top with egg white mixed with a little water. Put a pan of hot water on bottom shelf while baking. Bake at 350 degrees about 30 minutes. Bake until golden brown and sounds hollow when tapped.

Spoon Bread

1 cup corn meal
1 pint water*
½ teaspoon salt
3 tablespoons margarine
2 tablespoons sugar
3 eggs
1 cup cold milk

Stir corn meal into boiling water. Stir one minute and remove from heat. Add butter and sugar. Beat well. Add egg yolks and cold milk. Beat well. Whip egg whites until stiff and fold into mixture. Place in a 9" x 12" pan (well buttered). Bake at 450 degrees for 30 minutes.

* 1 pint = 2 cups

Special with fried or roasted chicken.

Lemon Pecan Bread

Cream 3/4 cup butter with 1½ cups sugar. Add 3 eggs, one at a time. Beat well after each addition. Combine 2¼ cups flour, ¼ teaspoon baking soda, ¼ teaspoon salt. Add to creamed mixture alternately with 3/4 cup buttermilk. Stir in 3/4 cup chopped pecans and 1 teaspoon grated lemon rind. Pour batter into greased and floured 9"x 5"x 3" loaf pan. Bake 350 degrees for 1 hour and 15 minutes. Cool for 10 minutes before removing from pan.

Buttermilk Biscuits

Sift 2 cups flour, ½ teaspoon salt, 1 tablespoon sugar, 2 teaspoons baking powder and ½ teaspoon baking soda. Cut ½ stick of margarine into it with a knife or use your hands. Then add 3/4 cup buttermilk. Blend into a ball. Roll out ½" thick. Cut into rounds using a cookie cutter or a glass. Bake at 400 degrees for 12 to 15 minutes.

Cream Cheese Braid

8 ounces sour cream, 1/2 cup sugar, 1/2 cup melted margarine, 1 teaspoon salt, 2 packages yeast, 1/2 cup warm water, 2 eggs, 4 cups flour.

Cream Cheese Filling: 8 ounces cream cheese, 3/4 cup sugar, 1 beaten egg, 1/8 teaspoon salt, 2 teaspoons vanilla. Combine all ingredients with a mixer until well blended.

Glaze: 2 cups powdered sugar, 1/4 cup milk, 2 teaspoons vanilla. Mix well.

Combine sour cream, sugar, margarine and salt. Mix well. Dissolve yeast in warm water in a mixing bowl. Stir in sour cream mixture and eggs. Add sifted flour. Mix well. Dough will be soft so cover tightly and chill overnight. Take out of refrigerator and divide into 4 equal portions. Knead each 4 or 5 times. Roll each into a 12" x 8" rectangle. Spread 1/4 of the filling on each piece. Roll up like a jelly roll - so its 12" long. Pinch ends together. Make 6 equal "X" cuts across the top of each loaf. Let rise until double in bulk. Bake at 350 degrees for 15-20 minutes. Spread with glaze while warm. Most delicious!

Popovers

1 cup flour, ½ teaspoon salt, 1 cup milk and 2 eggs.

Preheat oven to 450 degrees. Grease cups of popover or muffin pan. Place pan in oven and preheat until sizzling hot. In medium bowl sift flour and salt together. Add milk and eggs and beat with a mixer until smooth. This usually takes about 2 minutes. Pour batter into hot popover pan filling each cup about ½ full. Bake at 450 degrees for 15 minutes. Reduce heat to 375 degrees and bake for 15-20 minutes more. Do not open oven door while they are baking.

These are delicious and so simple! We like them with butter and jam.

Dumplings & Noodles

Hepaticas

In the spring on Sundays we always went for a walk in the woods to look for the first wildflowers. And one day there they would be, All of the little lavender-blue hepaticas peeping out from under the fallen leaves. Then we would know spring has come again. God's in his heaven, all is right with the world.

My daughter, Carol, loves hepaticas and all the wildflowers just like I do. When she was a little girl she had quite a walk to school, over the fields and woods. Hardly a day went by when she didn't come home with her hand behind her back with an offering for me. Queen Anne's lace, wild asters, daisies - we loved them all. One winter's day she came home with a tumbleweed covered with ice that looked just like crystal. I can still see her standing in the doorway holding it out to me.

Bread Dumplings

Toast 2 slices of bread and cut into small cubes. Take 1 cup flour, 1 egg, pinch of salt and enough water to make a soft dough. Mix in a small bowl. When smooth, stir in the bread cubes and mix well. Have a pot of boiling water ready to which you have added a teaspoon of salt. Use a tablespoon to cut spoonfuls of dough and drop into the boiling water. Cook until the dumplings float and are done. Take them out of the water with a slotted spoon and drain. Pour a little melted butter over them (about 1/4 cup). Delicious served with goulash, beef stew or pot roast. Serves four.

This recipe may be doubled if you need more.

Chicken Liver Dumplings

Chop a small onion very fine. Sauté in 1 tablespoon of margarine. Take off fire after it is slightly brown. It should only sauté for a few minutes. Stir in 1 chopped chicken liver. Add ½ cup bread crumbs, 1 egg, ½ teaspoon chopped parsley, a dash of salt and pepper. Mix well. The mixture should be firm enough to roll into little balls the size of marbles. Drop into boiling soup. Cook until they float. They are best in chicken soup.

Farina Dumplings

Take 1 egg and beat with a fork until frothy. Add a dash of salt and pepper. Add enough farina to make a stiff dough like putty. Mash in a teaspoon of butter. Let stand 5 minutes. Then cut tiny pieces (¼ teaspoon size) with a teaspoon and drop into boiling soup. Cook for about 5 minutes until they float. These are also most delicious in chicken soup.

Red Dumplings

Take 2 cups Flour, 1/2 teaspoon salt, 2 eggs, 1/2 cup cold mashed potatoes (potatoes optional) and enough water to make a stiff dough. Shape into a ball. In the meantime, put 1 tablespoon oil and 1 tablespoon margarine into a large frying pan. Slice 1 or 2 peeled potatoes thinly and fry lightly. Then sprinkle about 2 teaspoons paprika. Add 1 cup water and bring to a boil. Turn fire low and put the dumplings in. To make dumplings pinch off a teaspoon of dough and roll between your palms to the size of your your little finger.* Add 1/2 teaspoon salt to the boiling water and drop the dumplings in one at a time. When all the dough is used up, turn the fire low, cover with a lid and steam slowly. It should take 10 to 15 minutes. Turn them once or twice while steaming. When done serve with applesauce or lettuce with bacon dressing.

⌣

*You may have to flour your hands once in awhile when you are rolling the dumplings.

⌣

Hungarian Plum Dumplings

1 cup mashed potatoes, 2 cups flour, 1/4 teaspoon salt, 2 eggs, 12 plums, 1 cup of soft bread torn into small pieces the size of croutons, 1/4 cup margarine, 1 tablespoon oil.

Sift flour and salt into a mixing bowl. Add mashed potatoes and eggs. Mix well. You may have to add a small amount of water so it rolls out easily. Roll dough out to 1/4" thick. Cut into 12 squares of 2" x 2". Remove pits from plums. Insert 1 or 2 sugar cubes into plum cavity. Place each plum onto a dough square. Fold dough around the plum and seal it tightly by rolling it in your hands. Boil a pot of water with 1/2 tablespoon salt. Carefully drop dumplings into the boiling water. Let boil for 10 minutes. Drain. Make crispies by using 2-3 slices of bread and tearing off small pieces and frying in 1 tablespoon of oil until golden brown. Add 1/4 cup margarine. When melted roll dumplings in with this and serve hot. Must be made with fresh plums.

We love these and sometimes just eat them as a meal!

Potato Balls

Peel and cut 3 large baking potatoes. Cook in salted water until they are done. Put them through a ricer or a sieve. When cooled, add 1 cup flour, ½ cup bread crumbs, 2 eggs and a pinch of salt. Mix well. Shape into balls the size of golf balls. Drop into boiling salted water. Cook until they float and are done. Using 2 or 3 slices of bread make crispies by tearing off small pieces and frying in 1 tablespoon oil until golden brown. Add 1 tablespoon margarine for flavor. Sprinkle over the drained potato balls and serve.

Delicious with pot roast or beef stew.

Hungarian Cheese Noodles

Take 2 cups flour. Make a well in the center and add 2 eggs, pinch of salt and enough cold water to make a stiff dough. Make into 2 balls. Flour tabletop or noodle board and roll out each ball to about ⅛" thick. Put flakes (rolled out dough) on a clean towel and leave them to dry about ½ hour. In the meantime, mix 1 pound cottage cheese, pinch salt, dash of pepper and 1 teaspoon sugar. Set aside. When flakes are dry sprinkle with flour. Cut into 3" strips. Lay one on top of another and cut ½" to make noodles. Boil water with ½ tablespoon of salt. Drop noodles into the boiling water. Boil about 5 minutes. Drain. Place noodles into a bowl with the cottage cheese mixture. Combine. Using 2 or 3 slices of bread make crispies by tearing off small pieces and frying in 1 tablespoon oil until golden brown. Add 1 tablespoon margarine for flavor. Sprinkle over noodles. You may also sprinkle with some more sugar. A surprisingly delicious dish!

～

You can make this recipe with packaged noodles if you don't have the time to make your own.

Soup from Cheese Noodles

After you have fried the croutons for the noodles, leave a few croutons and a little oil/margarine mixture in the pan. Sprinkle ½ teaspoon paprika and add 1 cup milk. Bring to a boil and then add to the water which the noodles were boiled in. Add a chicken bouillon cube and some noodles. Presto – an unusually delicious soup!

You can boil 1 or 2 peeled, thinly sliced potatoes in the water the noodles were cooked in. It makes the soup thicker and some can be mixed in with the cheese noodles.

Cabbage Noodles

Use this as an alternate to the cottage cheese mixture. Shred 1 small cabbage. Sprinkle ¼ teaspoon salt and pepper. Heat oil in a frying pan. When hot, add cabbage. Cover and steam on low heat for about 10 minutes stirring frequently. If dry, add 1 tablespoon water. Mix with noodles. Drizzle with butter and sprinkle with croutons.

Macaroni and Cheese

Cook ½ box of elbow macaroni and drain. Put into a square baking pan. For the cheese sauce melt ½ stick margarine in a frying pan. Add 2 tablespoons flour. Mix well. Add 1 chicken bouillon cube dissolved in 1 cup boiling water. Stir. Add 2 cups milk Mix well. Add assorted cheeses. I usually use about ½ brick of sharp cheddar cheese and some parmesan. Slice it in. Stir and it melts quickly. A few slices of Swiss adds a nice flavor and smooth texture. Salt and pepper to taste. Add ½ chopped fresh or canned tomato. Pour the cheese sauce over the macaroni.

Using 2-3 slices of bread, make crispies by tearing off small pieces and frying in 1 tablespoon of oil until golden brown. Remove crispies. Add 1 tablespoon of margarine (for flavor) to the oil. Drizzle this over the macaroni and cheese. Sprinkle crispies on top. Bake for ½ hour (uncovered) or until hot at 350 degrees.

Appetizers & Salads

Daisies

In the summer on our Sunday drives we would always come upon a field full of daisies. Their pretty delicate white flowers sprinkled through the grass always tempted me. My husband would stop while I picked a bouquet. They are so long lasting. I could enjoy them all week.

Cheese Squares

Take 6 slices of bread. Cut off crusts and cut each slice in half. Toast lightly. Whip the whites of 2 eggs until stiff. Fold in 4 ounces of grated parmesan cheese. Spread over the toasted squares. Put a strip of fried bacon on top of each square. Put in the oven for a few minutes until puffed and golden brown. Serve immediately. Serves six.

Toast Squares

Take a loaf of unsliced bread and cut off crust. Cut bread into 1" squares. If you can't get an unsliced loaf, cut slices into 4 squares. Melt ¼ pound margarine and pour over the squares. Fluff the squares until margarine is evenly distributed. Sprinkle with 2 tablespoons sesame seeds and ½ cup grated parmesan cheese. Fluff with these 2 ingredients until the squares are coated. If necessary add more margarine. Spread on a cookie sheet. Bake at 350 degrees for about 10 minutes until golden brown.

Blue Cheese and Olive Ball

8 ounces Philadelphia Brand cream cheese (plain or whipped), 3 tablespoons butter, 1 tablespoon brandy, 1 - 4 ounce package of blue cheese, 1 tablespoon chives, ¼ cup chopped olives, 1 cup chopped pecans, 1 tablespoon chopped parsley. Parsley sprig and olives for garnish.

Combine first 3 ingredients. Add crumbled blue cheese. Mix well. Stir in chives and olives. In a separate bowl mix pecans and parsley. Using plastic wrap form cheese mixture into a ball. Roll in pecan and parsley mixture so the cheese is completely coated. Refrigerate. Garnish with parsley and olives.

This is a delicious appetizer which we always serve with Pepperidge Farm crackers.

Liver Paté

Take 1 pound fresh chicken livers. Wash well in salted water and drain. Put a tablespoon each of oil and margarine into a frying pan. Add 1 finely chopped onion and brown until golden. Add the drained chicken livers. Put a lid on and simmer until done and the juices are cooked away. Remove from pan. Put through a food processor or mash with a fork.

Cook 3 eggs, making hard boiled eggs. Peel and cool. Mash well with a fork. Add to chicken liver. Salt and pepper to taste. Add 2 tablespoons salad dressing and mix well. A pinch of thyme and 2 strips of bacon fried and ground adds a delicious flavor to the liver paté.

We serve these with crackers for all of our holidays and they are really good!

Tea Sandwiches

For these we use Pepperidge Farm white sandwich bread and whole wheat bread with the crusts removed.

Chicken Salad: Use 1 cup of chicken breast cooked the same as in the chicken soup recipe. Add ¼ cup finely chopped celery, 1 teaspoon finely grated onion, ¼ cup Miracle Whip salad dressing thinned with a little milk. Toss together and salt and pepper to taste. Spread over white bread. Cut sandwich into 3 "fingers."

Ham Salad: Use 1 cup chopped ham, finely chopped small sweet pickle, ¼ cup finely chopped celery, 1 teaspoon finely grated onion, a small amount, "knife point" measure of mustard, ¼ cup Miracle Whip salad dressing thinned with a little milk. Toss together and salt and pepper to taste. Spread small amount on white bread. Cut sandwich into 3 "fingers."

Cucumber: Lightly salt thinly sliced cucumber. Butter white bread and place a thin layer of cucumber on to make a delicate sandwich. Cut sandwich into 3 "fingers."

38

Egg Salad: Peel 3 hard boiled eggs and mash with a fork. Add salt and pepper, "knife point" small measure of mustard, 1 small sweet pickle finely diced and ¼ cup Miracle Whip salad dressing. Spread on whole wheat bread. Cut sandwich into 3 "fingers".

Cream Cheese with Watercress: Wash and dry with paper towels the sprigs of watercress. Spread cream cheese on whole wheat bread. Top with a thin layer of watercress. Cut sandwich into 3 "fingers".

Date and Nut: Buy the cans (1 or 2 should be enough for a small luncheon when served with all of the other sandwiches) of date and nut bread. Cut into thin circles. Spread with cream cheese. Make sandwich and cut in half.

∽

All of these sandwiches are so simple and delicious. We love to make them for a wedding or baby shower. They look very elegant when served on a pretty serving tray.

∽

Homemade Pizza

Dissolve 1 package of yeast in 2 tablespoons warm water. Mix 1 cup very warm water, 2 tablespoons ~~salad~~ *olive* oil, 1 teaspoon salt, 3 cups flour and the dissolved yeast. Knead together until smooth. Put into a bowl and spread a little oil over the dough. Cover and let rise until double. Take out of bowl and knead. Make into 2 balls. Roll each out to about 12" square or round. Put on a well oiled pizza pan or cookie sheet. Cover with tomato sauce. Sprinkle with garlic powder, a little pepper, and shredded mozzarella cheese. Then sprinkle some oregano over all. You can also add sausage or pepperoni if preferred. Bake at 350 degrees for 20 minutes.

Bacon Dressing for Salads

Take about 4 strips of bacon and cut into 1/4" pieces. Fry until pale brown. Take out bacon. To the bacon fat add 1/4 cup vinegar, 1/2 cup water, pinch salt, sprinkle black pepper and 2 to 3 tablespoons sugar according to taste. Bring to a boil and then shut off fire. You may have to add more vinegar or water. Taste it and see if it needs it. Add the bacon and cool to room temperature. This is special on garden lettuce, endive or potato salad.

AUNT MAY'S

Aunt Mary's Salad Dressing

Use a 1/2 pint jar with a lid. In the jar add 1 clove garlic (cut into quarters), 1 tablespoon sugar, 1/4 teaspoon salt, dash of pepper, 1/2 cup salad oil, 1/4 cup vinegar, 1 tablespoon ketchup, and a pinch of oregano. Put the lid on and shake until thick. This is a great favorite with our family. You can make it sweeter or more sour by adding more or less vinegar. Keep in mind that many of these recipes are seasoned to taste.

Cucumber Salad

Take a large cucumber, peel and slice thinly. Put into a bowl and salt lightly. Leave stand for about ½ an hour. Then press the slices between your hands to press out all of the water. Put the pressed slices into a bowl and add ½ tablespoon minced onions, 1 clove minced garlic, 1 tablespoon chopped parsley, 1 teaspoon sugar, 2 tablespoons vinegar, 1 tablespoon oil, and a heaping tablespoon sour cream. Mix well. Sprinkle with paprika and serve. + tumeric!

String Bean Salad

French one pound of fresh green beans. Cook in salted water until done but not too soft or soggy. Drain and put in a bowl. Add about one tablespoon sugar, sprinkle of pepper, ¼ cup salad oil, and ¼ cup vinegar. Finely chop one tablespoon onion, one tablespoon fresh parsley and one garlic clove. Toss all ingredients to-gether lightly until mixed well. Serve hot or cold.

Grandma Olson Klund's
German Potato Salad * ♡

5 slices bacon, 1 medium onion finely chopped, 1/4 cup vinegar, 1/4 cup salad oil, 1 tablespoon sugar, 1/2 teaspoon salt, 1/8 teaspoon pepper, 5 med. cooked red skin potatoes, 1/4 cup chopped celery, 2 tablespoons chopped parsley. ♡

Cut bacon into 1/4" pieces and fry until crisp. Remove and place on a paper towel. Reserve drippings. Boil potatoes in their skins until soft and cooked. Peel and slice them. Add salt, pepper, celery, sugar, salad oil, onion, bacon, parsley, vinegar and 2 table-spoons bacon fat. (drippings). Fluff together with 2 forks. Serve on lettuce leaves.

Southern Potato Salad

Boil 5 med. potatoes in their skins until done. Peel and slice. Add 1/4 cup chopped celery, 2 small sweet pickles cubed, 1 chopped hard boiled egg, 1 chopped small onion, 2 tablespoons chopped parsley. Take 1/2 cup salad dressing, 1 tablespoon sour cream, 1 tablespoon vinegar and stir together. Season potatoes with salt, pepper and a teaspoon of sugar. Pour the dressing mixture in with other ingredients and fluff together with 2 forks. Sprinkle with parsley.

Cole Slaw with Cooked Dressing

Slice a small head of cabbage very thinly to look like fine noodles. Do not shred. Sprinkle with salt and pepper. Set aside.

Take ½ cup vinegar, ½ cup sugar and ¼ cup butter or margarine and put in a pan and bring to a boil. Take 2 egg yolks and beat together with a fork. Very gently pour the boiling vinegar mixture over them stirring constantly. Put back on the stove and cook over a low fire until it thickens. Take off the stove and pour over cabbage. Fluff it all together and refrigerate.

This is so good to serve with a plum tomato cut into 4 wedges with the slaw in the middle on a lettuce leaf.

Fruit Cup

Cut 1 grapefruit and 2 oranges into bite sized pieces. Cut 1 banana in half lengthwise and slice. Add this to 1 can of fruit cocktail. Mix together with 1 tablespoon brandy. Top individual servings with frosted grapes or sherbet. Very appetizing!

Frosted Grapes

Rinse and dry grapes. Pull apart into small clusters. Take an egg white and whip until frothy. Dip grapes into egg white and then into granulated sugar. Let them dry on a paper towel.

∽

These are nice to serve at a party either on their own or as a garnish to fruit cup.

∽

Waldorf Salad

Peel 2 apples. Core and dice them. Cut up 2 stalks of celery into small cubes. Add ¼ cup chopped walnuts and ¼ cup raisins. In a separate bowl mix together ¼ cup Miracle Whip salad dressing, a heaping tablespoon sour cream and a little milk to thin it out. Pour this mixture over other ingredients and fluff together. Serve on a lettuce leaf. This is nice to make for a luncheon or wedding shower.

∽

Fruit and Jello Mold

Take a 16 ounce can of fruit cocktail and drain, saving the juice. Prepare jello as directed on package except use the fruit juice as part of the required liquid. Let jello stand in refrigerator until slightly thickened. Add fruit cocktail by folding into the jello. Put into jello mold (you can use 1 large one or small individual servings). I like to use small heart shaped molds. Put back into refrigerator and chill for at least 2 hours. Unmold by dipping the bottom into hot water for a few seconds. Serve on lettuce leaves. You can change the color according to the occasion - red for Valentine's Day, green for St. Patrick's Day, yellow for Easter.

For topping: make a mixture of 8 ounces of cream cheese, 1 tablespoon sugar, 1 teaspoon vanilla and enough milk to make it the consistency of whipped cream. Place a spoonful on top of each serving. You may garnish with a strawberry or cherry.

A favorite holiday dessert. This looks very festive and is delicious.

Meats & Vegetables

The Family Crest

   Our family crest was something we all cherished. My father-in-law, Freidrich von Hohen, brought it with him from the old country, but it was lost when his things were put in storage. He lived with us for awhile and what a great storyteller he was! My children were fascinated as he told of his exploits as a Hussar in the Prussian Army. As they grew up the family crest was always a reminder of him. Many years later my daughters had it researched and a reproduction was made. They gave it to my husband and me for a Christmas present. We had our family crest back again!

Hungarian Goulash

Put 1 tablespoon oil in a pan. Finely slice 1 large onion and fry in oil until golden brown. Add 1 teaspoon paprika. Stir it around and add the meat. You can use chicken, beef or veal. We always like breast and shank of veal. Add a piece of green pepper, a stalk of celery, a tomato (fresh or canned), 1 bay leaf, and 2 cloves. Salt and pepper to taste. Steam the meat until it draws juice. Then sprinkle 1 tablespoon of flour on the meat. Add 1 or 2 cups of water and simmer until tender. This usually takes about 2 hours. Add 1 or 2 diced potatoes for the last 1/2 hour. I like to serve this with rice, noodles or bread dumplings.

This is a simple but very delicious meal.

Mother's Pot Roast

For this recipe use a 3-4 pound roast of beef. They are tender and good for slicing. Wipe meat off with a paper towel. Measure 1 tablespoon flour, 1 teaspoon salt, dash of black pepper, and a pinch of ginger. Mix well. Rub this mixture on all sides of the meat. Melt a little oil in a heavy pot and brown the meat on all sides. Then add 1 large sliced onion, 1 clove garlic, 2 stalks celery, a piece of green pepper, 1 tomato, 2 carrots, and a piece of yellow turnip. Put vegetables all around the roast. Add 1/4 cup water and 1/4 cup wine or sherry. Put the lid on and simmer or roast in the oven about 3 hours. For the gravy: Remove meat. To the essence in the pan add a heaping tablespoon flour. Mix well. Add 1 to 2 cups water. Cook until thick. Strain gravy (including all of the vegetables) through a sieve. Makes a most delicious gravy!

∽

Serve with potato balls or homemade noodles.

∽

Chicken Pie

Cut up a stewing or frying chicken and wash well under running water. Put pieces in a 4 qt. pot and fill 3/4 full with water. Add 2 carrots, 2 stalks celery, a tomato, 1 onion, 1 bay leaf, sprig of parsley, sprig of thyme, 1 tablespoon salt and a dash of pepper. Simmer until it's done, about 2 hours. Take chicken from broth and cool.

Peel and dice 2 potatoes. Boil in water with 1/2 teaspoon salt. When covered with a lid, they should be cooked in 1/2 an hour. Drain.

Cut chicken into bite sized pieces. Add potatoes, cut up carrots from broth, and a cup of cooked or canned peas. In a saucepan melt 1 generous tablespoon of margarine. Add 1 heaping tablespoon flour. Mix well. Add 2 cups of chicken broth. If too thick, add more broth. Place the chicken and vegetables in a pie plate. Pour sauce over. Top with pie crust (recipe in dessert section) Bake until golden brown at 350 degrees for 1 hour.

Brunswick Stew

Take 2 pounds of chicken, 2 carrots, a stalk of celery and 1 onion and cook in a pot of water with 1/2 tablespoon of salt for about 1½ hours until meat is tender. Remove chicken. When cool, cut chicken into small pieces. Remove carrots and slice. Strain broth into another pot. Add 3 chopped fresh tomatoes, (fresh or canned), 1 cup green lima beans, 3 peeled and cubed potatoes, 1 tablespoon sugar, salt and pepper to taste. Cook until potatoes are tender, about 20 minutes. Add the meat and 1 cup corn (cut from the cob or frozen). Add 1 tablespoon butter. Cook 5 minutes. Serves 6-8. Serve with rolls or Italian bread.

Lamb Stew

You can use neck of lamb, shoulder chops or even lamb shanks. Rinse the meat. Put it in a stew pot with enough water to cover it well. Put on to boil then add a sliced onion, clove of garlic, 2 carrots sliced, a fresh tomato diced or ¼ cup canned tomato, sprig of thyme, ½ a turnip diced, 2 cloves, a bay leaf, 1 teaspoon salt and sprinkle of pepper. Let simmer for about 1 hour. Add 2 or 3 peeled and diced potatoes. I like to add a handful of lima beans or peas. When potatoes are cooked thicken with a tablespoon of flour mixed with a little water.

We always have this with Oatmeal Bannock.

Soup Meat Casserole

I use beef shin meat and make beef noodle soup using the same recipe as chicken noodle soup. Cook until the meat is tender. This usually takes 2-3 hours. Take the meat out to use in the casserole.

Chop the meat finely. Add 1 minced onion, 1/2 minced garlic clove, salt and pepper - a dash of each according to taste, 1 beaten egg and 2 or 3 tablespoons of the broth. Mix well with a fork.

Cook 1 cup of rice. I like to use Carolina. Put a layer of rice in a casserole, a layer of meat, another of rice and another of meat. Make bread croutons using 2 or 3 slices. Pull off small pieces to make the croutons and fry until golden brown in 1/2 tablespoon each of oil and margarine. Dot top of casserole with butter and sprinkle with croutons. Bake 1 hour at 350.

Tomato Sauce: melt 1 tablespoon margarine, add 1 tablespoon flour and mix well. Add a can of tomato sauce and cook until thickened. Season to taste with salt, pepper and sugar. Serve over individual portions of casserole.

Rouladen

1 pound ground meat, 10 crushed Saltine crackers, 1/2 finely chopped onion, finely chopped garlic clove, 1 teaspoon each of chopped parsley and celery top, dash of thyme, 1/2 teaspoon salt, pepper to taste and 1 egg. Mix well.

Use a package of 6-8 pieces of chipped steak. Take a slice and put a ball of the meat mixture in the center. Roll up the steak to completely cover the meat. Fasten with tooth-picks or by tying with a string. Heat oil in a frying pan (enough to cover the bottom of pan). Fry rouladens until brown on all sides. Take out and put on a baking pan. Add a tablespoon of wine and a little water to the essence left in frying pan. Pour into baking pan. Cover with foil and bake for 1/2 hour at 350 degrees. To make gravy add a tablespoon of flour to the essence in the pan. Add 1 cup water and cook until thickened. If you like you may add a tablespoon of sour cream or white wine to the gravy. Season to taste. Pour over the rouladens.

Roast Chicken or Goose

Wash and dry the bird. Rub with salt and sprinkle with pepper inside and out. Make the stuffing recipe using the chopped liver. Prick the skin all over to release the fat while roasting. Cover and roast for 2-3 hours at 350 degrees until brown and well done. Uncover for the last hour. <u>To make gravy</u>: Remove bird from pan. Pour off most of the fat. Add 2 tablespoons flour to the essence remaining in the pan. Mix well. Over a medium heat add water and stir until it is the right consistency. Salt and pepper to taste.

Stuffing for Poultry

Take 4 slices of stale bread. Soak for a minute in cold water. Press the water out in your hands until the bread is as dry as possible.

Take a tablespoon of margarine and put in a small frying pan. Add ½ finely chopped onion and a minced clove of garlic. Cook until onion is pale brown. Add chopped chicken or turkey liver, a tablespoon chopped parsley, salt and pepper. Take off fire. Add to the pressed out bread. Add 1 egg and mix well. Put into chicken or turkey cavity. I like to add a little poultry seasoning and thyme with the stuffing.

Fried Chicken

Wash and dry chicken pieces. Sprinkle with salt and pepper. Combine a mixture of ½ cup flour, ¼ teaspoon salt, sprinkle of pepper and a dash of paprika. Dip each piece into this flour mixture. Make a mixture of 1 egg beaten with 4 tablespoons milk. Dip floured chicken into this and then into fine bread crumbs. Let stand for 1 hour. Fry in deep fat until golden brown. Drain well on paper towels so it is not greasy. Put chicken pieces on a baking sheet, cover with foil and bake ½ hour at 350 degrees.

Roast Lamb or Pork

These are made the same except you must remove all the skin and fat from the lamb. Rub meat with salt and pepper. Make little cuts and insert pieces of garlic. Cover with sliced onion. Around sides add carrots, celery, piece of pepper, sprig of thyme or rosemary, ¼ cup water and 1 cubed tomato. Cover and bake at 350 degrees for 2-3 hours until tender. Remove meat. Put pan over medium heat, add heaping tablespoon flour to essence, stir, add 1 cup water. Cook until thickened and strain. Delicious!

Pork Chops Creole

6 - 1" pork chops, 1 chopped onion, ½ chopped green pepper, 1 tablespoon oil, 1 teaspoon salt, ¼ teaspoon pepper, 1 teaspoon sugar, 1½ teaspoons Worcestershire sauce, 1 cup uncooked rice, 1 large can tomatoes.

Wipe pork chops off with a paper towel. Season with salt and pepper on each side. You can also use some garlic powder if you like. Brown chops in oil in a frying pan. This should take about 10 minutes. Make sure to brown each side. Remove chops and set aside. Saute onions and peppers in the same frying pan. Add tomatoes, salt, pepper, sugar and Worcestershire sauce. Cook about 10 minutes. Place chops in a baking pan. Pour tomato sauce over chops and bake uncovered at 350 degrees for ½ hour.

Cook 1 cup of rice. Serve pork chops on a bed of rice with tomato sauce poured over it.

Crab Cakes

1 pound fresh crabmeat, drained and flaked,
1/4 cup melted margarine, 2 tablespoons minced
green peppers, 1/4 cup minced onion, 3/4 cup fine
dry breadcrumbs, 1 beaten egg, 1 tablespoon each
of salad dressing, dried parsley flakes, and
lemon juice, 1 teaspoon each of Worcestershire
sauce, Old Bay seasoning and dry mustard.
Dash of red pepper, 1/4 - 1/2 cup fine dry breadcrumbs and vegetable oil.

Saute onion and green pepper in margarine
until tender. Remove from heat. Stir in crabmeat
and next 9 ingredients. Mix well. Shape into 8
patties. Coat with additional breadcrumbs.
Pour oil to depth of 1/4" into heavy skillet.
Fry cakes in hot oil (315 degrees) for 4 to 5
minutes on each side.

Shrimp with Garlic Rice

Shell and clean about a pound of shrimp. Place evenly in a baking pan or on a cookie sheet. Mince 3-4 garlic cloves. Melt ½ stick of margarine over medium heat. Add the garlic and let it cook about 1-2 minutes. With a spoon drizzle this over the shrimp. Sprinkle with 2-3 tablespoons of sherry and the juice of 1 lemon. Dust lightly with paprika. Bake at 350 degrees, uncovered, for 8-10 minutes or until shrimp are pink/white and done.

For the rice: Cook 1 cup of rice. Rinse well and steam it. Mince 2-3 garlic cloves. Melt ½ stick butter or margarine over medium heat. Add the garlic and let it cook for 1-2 minutes. Drizzle over the rice with 1 tablespoon chopped fresh parsley. Mix by fluffing together using 2 forks. Serve shrimp on a bed of rice. A simple and delicious meal!

You can add extra "zest" to the rice by adding 1 teaspoon grated lemon peel.

Sweet and Sour Meatloaf

Take 1 pound ground meat, 1 grated onion, 12 crushed saltine crackers, a pinch pepper, ½ teaspoon salt, 2 egg whites, and ½ can (8 oz.) tomato sauce. Mix well. Shape into a loaf. Put a strip of bacon on top.

Take 2 tablespoons vinegar, ¼ teaspoon mustard, ½ can (8 oz.) tomato sauce, 2 tablespoons brown sugar and ⅔ cup water. Mix well. Pour over the meatloaf. Bake 350 degrees for 1 to 1½ hours.

Creamed Dried Beef

Take 1 package (1/4 pound) dried beef and pick it apart into small pieces. Place it into a dish and pour water over it. Take out and squeeze dry. This makes it much less salty. Put a good tablespoon margarine in a frying pan. When hot add the dried beef and stir until it frizzles up. Then add a good tablespoon flour. Stir it in well. Add 1 cup milk and 1/2 cup water boiled with chicken bouillon. If too thick add more milk. It should be a nice creamy sauce. Then I like to add 1 sliced hard boiled egg and 2 tablespoons cooked peas. Pour over buttered toast squares. It really looks good and tastes special.

Hungarian Peasant Meal

One thing we had lots of times for dinner was this meal. My mother told us in the old country they called potatoes "feld hendles", field chickens, as they took the place of meat.

Boil ½ dozen red new potatoes in their jackets for about ½ hour or less until soft. Mix 1 pound cottage cheese with a sprinkle of salt, pepper and paprika. Add a heaping tablespoon sour cream and ½ cup chopped scallions. Toss this all together.

Serve potatoes in their jackets. We just peeled them on our plate, sprinkle with salt and pepper and a lump of butter. Serve with a couple of spoonfuls of the cottage cheese mixture.

∽

This really is very tasty and I still make it once in awhile when I get a yen for it. It's healthy too!

∽

Sauces for Boiled Meats
Dill Sauce

Melt 1 tablespoon margarine in a pan. Add
1 teaspoon finely chopped onion and cook lightly.
Then add 1 heaping tablespoon flour and blend.
Add 2 tablespoons of chopped fresh dill. Stir.
Add 1½ cups chicken bouillon and bring to a boil.
When thick add a pinch of salt, sprinkle of
pepper, 1 tablespoon sugar, 1 tablespoon vinegar,
(or vinegar to taste). Take off heat. Then stir
in a large tablespoon sour cream and serve.

Gooseberry Sauce

Melt 1 tablespoon margarine in a pan.
Add a heaping tablespoon flour and blend.
Then add 1 cup gooseberries and ¼ cup water.
Bring to a boil. Add sugar to taste. Add a
pinch of salt and a heaping tablespoon sour
cream.

Horseradish Sauce

Take a jar of grated horseradish and put contents in a fine muslin cloth and press out the juice. If you want you can just press in your hands. Put horseradish in a bowl. Add ½ cup hot chicken bouillon and 1 teaspoon sugar (or more to taste). Add a large dollop of sour cream and mix well.

All sauces can be used with boiled beef or chicken. Delicious!

Sauteed Cabbage

Put 2 tablespoons oil in a frying pan. Add 1 head of shredded cabbage and a shredded tart apple. Add about one teaspoon salt, one tablespoon brown sugar and pepper to taste. Cover and steam over low heat until tender, about ten minutes. Stir frequently as it scorches easily. When done add a tablespoon or so of vinegar. If not tasty enough add a little more sugar and vinegar.

Fried Tomatoes

Take 3 nice size tomatoes - not too ripe. Cut off ends. Cut each tomato into 3 thick slices. On top of each slice sprinkle salt, pepper and 1/2 teaspoon sugar. Then dip each slice in bread crumbs. Put about 1 tablespoon of each oil and margarine in a frying pan. When hot, place the tomato slices in the pan. Fry sugar side up first because sugar burns very easily. Fry each side golden brown. Put slices on a serving platter. If there is no more shortening in the pan, put in 1 tablespoon of margarine. Add 1/2 tablespoon flour. Add about a cup of milk to make a thin sauce. The bread crumbs left in the pan really add to the flavor. Salt and pepper to taste. Pour over the tomato slices.

Delicious!

Zucchini in Tomato Sauce
"Zuspice"

Peel and shred 2 zucchini. Add a teaspoon salt. Mix and let set about 1 hour. Put 1 tablespoon oil in a frying pan. When hot brown 1 minced onion. Add 1 tablespoon flour and mix well. Add 1 - #2 can tomato sauce mixed with ½ cup water.* When this mixture is boiling take the zucchini, squeeze the water from it, and add to the tomato sauce. Cook until done. This usually takes about 15 to 20 minutes. Cook on a slow heat so it doesn't burn. Add a tablespoon of sugar or more to taste. A piece of green pepper cooked with it is very good.

My mother always served this with fried chicken and spoon bread.

*If you would like it a little spicy, add 1 bay leaf and 1 clove.

Creamed Vegetables

<u>Peas and Carrots</u>: Use 1 package frozen or 1 can of peas and 3-4 sliced carrots.

<u>Cauliflower</u>: Use 1 head cut into small pieces.

<u>Kohlrabi</u>: Use 3-6 peeled and cut into chunks.

Steam vegetables in salted water until done to your liking. For peas use directions on box or can. To make cream sauce melt a tablespoon of butter or margarine in a pan. Add a tablespoon of flour and blend well. Add ½ cup of the vegetable water and ½ cup milk. If too thick add more milk. Season with salt and pepper. Add the vegetables. Warm again and serve. For the cauliflower and Kohlrabi I like to add a dash of mace.

<u>Sucotash</u>: Put 1 cup of water in a pan. Add a pinch of sugar and a package of large lima beans. Cook until beans are tender. Add a good tablespoon of butter, ½ tablespoon flour, 3-4 ears of corn cut off the cob or 1 bag of frozen corn, and ½ cup milk. Cook until thick and corn is done, about 5 minutes. Season with salt and fresh ground pepper.

Creamed Spinach

Cook your fresh or frozen spinach in a little salted water until tender. Strain and chop fine. In a saucepan put a large table-spoon margarine. Add a tablespoon or so of finely chopped onion and finely chopped clove of garlic. Sauté lightly. Add a tablespoon of flour. Stir. Then add 1 cup milk and 1/4 cup spinach water. Stir and cook until creamy. Add a dash of pepper, salt and pinch of mace. Then add the spinach and stir until well blended. A 1/2 cup of ham broth instead of spinach water is especially delicious.

Relish

Grind 15 green tomatoes, 1 doz. red and green peppers and 2 large onions. Add 2 1/2 pints vinegar, 2 pints sugar, 2 tablespoons mustard seed, 1 tablespoon celery seed, 2 tablespoons whole cloves, 2 tablespoons salt and 2 cinnamon sticks. Mix in a large pot and bring to a boil. Boil for 15 minutes. Take out cloves and cinnamon sticks. Put in hot sterilized pint jars and seal. Very tasty with sausage and hot dogs.

Corn and Apple Fritters

Cut off the kernels of 3 ears of fresh corn. You can use frozen but fresh is better. Sift 3/4 cup flour, with 1 teaspoon baking powder, 1/4 teaspoon salt, pinch paprika. Add 1 egg yolk and 1/4 cup milk. Mix well. Add the corn. Beat the egg white until stiff. Fold into the corn mixture. Drop carefully by tablespoon into hot oil on medium heat. They should look flat and round about the size of a silver dollar pancake. Fry on each side until golden brown. Drain on a paper towel.

You can use this same recipe and use 1 cup shredded apples instead of the corn. Apple fritters are good when sprinkled with powdered sugar.

Candied Sweet Potatoes

Boil sweet potatoes in salted water until soft and done. Remove skins and cut into 1" slices. Place slices in a buttered baking pan. Sprinkle with salt, pepper, 1 cup brown sugar and 1/2 cup Karo syrup. Dot with butter. Bake about 1/2 hour until glazed.

Parsley Potatoes

I use small red new potatoes, maybe a dozen or so. Use as many as you think you will need. Boil in salted water until soft and done. Peel and slice in half. Put in a frying pan with ½ stick of butter over medium heat. When heated through sprinkle with salt and pepper and a tablespoon of chopped parsley.

Twice Baked Potatoes

Use Idaho potatoes and bake for about 1 hour until done. Before baking wash them and puncture a few times with a knife. When done slice the top off and with a teaspoon remove the inside and put into a bowl. After all the potatoes are hollowed out and insides are all in the bowl, add ½ stick butter, salt, pepper and enough milk to make them fluffy. Put back into the skins heaped up nicely and sprinkled with paprika. You can also add some Parmesan cheese. Put them back in the oven and re-bake at 350 degrees until hot.

Desserts

Violets

When I was a young girl and working I had Thursdays off. I always went downtown (Philadelphia) to do a little shopping and take in a matinee. Every spring there they would be the flower ladies. They sat on the sidewalk with their buckets of wildflowers. They had corsages of violets, gardenias and trailing arbutus. I loved the violets, such a lovely blue with the heart spread of leaves. They were only a quarter a bunch. I'd pin them on my dress and the day became special. The world was beautiful!

Philadelphia

Brandied Peaches

Take about 6 nice ripe yellow peaches and put them into a bowl. Pour boiling water over them. Let stand for a few minutes. Peel the skins off. It should peel off easily. Take 2 cups water and 1 cup sugar. Bring to a boil. Drop the peeled peaches in and simmer until done. About 10 minutes. Then take the peaches out and put them in a bowl. Boil the remaining syrup down a little and add a jigger of Southern Comfort. Pour over peaches and chill before serving.

Using the boiling water then peeling the peaches leaves all the pink under the skin. Cooking them whole with the pits intact gives them a very special flavor. I serve this in a sherbet glass pouring the syrup over the peaches. It always looks quite elegant!

Most enjoyable!

Spanish Cream

In a saucepan mix 1 envelope gelatin, a few grains of salt, 2 tablespoons sugar and 2 beaten egg yolks. Add 1 cup of hot milk slowly. Cook and stir over slow fire until gelatin dissolves. This takes about 5 minutes. Take off the stove. Add 1 cup milk and 1 teaspoon vanilla. Chill until slightly firm.

Beat the 2 egg whites until they peak. Then fold in 1/4 cup sugar a little at a time. Fold into the gelatin mixture and pour into a mold. Chill.

You can add some rum and nutmeg and it will taste like eggnog.

This is a very delicate dessert that everyone loves!

Rice Pudding with Wine Sauce

Take 3 eggs and beat until frothy. Add ½ cup sugar, pinch of salt and 1 teaspoon of vanilla. Add 3 cups milk and mix well. To this mixture add 2 cups of cooked and drained rice. Pour into a casserole dish. Sprinkle with nutmeg and place casserole dish in a pan of water. Bake 1 hour at 350 degrees.

Wine sauce: Take 3/4 cup red sweet wine, 3/4 cup water and ½ cup sugar. Bring to a boil in a saucepan. Thicken with a tablespoon of corn starch diluted in a small amount of water. It should be thick, smooth and easy to pour. Cool and spoon over individual servings of the baked rice pudding.

Delicious!

Floating Islands

Mix 2 cups milk in a frying pan with 2 tablespoons sugar and a pinch of salt. Bring to a slow boil. In the meantime beat 2 egg whites until stiff. Add 2 tablespoons sugar slowly and beat until they peak. When the milk is slowly boiling take a tablespoon of the egg white mixture and put it in the boiling milk. Make the rest of the "islands" the same way until all of the egg whites are used up. Have heat on simmer. Cover and simmer for 5 minutes. Remove lid and flip the islands to the other side. Cover and let stand for 5 minutes. Remove islands with a slotted spoon. Put in a serving bowl. Take 2 egg yolks, 1 tablespoon corn starch, 1 tablespoon sugar, and beat with 2 tablespoons of cold milk. Slowly add the hot milk from the frying pan. After mixing, pour back into the pan and cook on medium heat until thick. Flavor the pudding with a teaspoon vanilla. Pour over the islands and chill. This looks especially nice served in a pretty bowl.

You can melt some sugar for a delicious carmel sauce (which hardens) to drizzle on top.

Spiced Stewed Pears

Peel 6 pears. I prefer Bartlett. Cut each in half and core. Make a syrup of 2 cups water, 1 cup sugar, 1 teaspoon vinegar, 3 cloves and a cinnamon stick. Bring syrup to a boil. Add pears and simmer 15-20 minutes until tender. Put pears in a bowl. Add 1 tablespoon brandy or rum to syrup and pour over pears. Chill before serving. *This is a delicious summer dessert!*

Bread Pudding

Beat 3 eggs with 1/3 cup sugar, pinch of salt, 3 cups milk and a teaspoon vanilla. Butter 4 slices of white bread. Cut off crusts and cut the bread into 1" cubes.

Pour egg mixture into baking pan. Add the bread cubes and poke them into the custard. Sprinkle a little mace over the top. Put pan into another pan which has 1" of water in it. Bake at 350 degrees for about 1 hour until set.

You may add some raisins and also use nutmeg instead of mace if preferred.

Baked Crepes

Take 2 eggs and beat until frothy. Add 2 tablespoons sugar, 1/8 teaspoon salt, 1 cup flour and 1 cup milk. Beat until smooth.

Have an 8" frying pan hot, seasoned with a little oil and butter mixture. Pour a small amount of batter (about 2 tablespoons) into the pan and spread very thin with a spoon. Turn once, they should be just pale brown. Each side should take no more than a minute on medium heat. Stack on a plate. When crepes are done, make the filling.

For the filling: Combine 1 pound cottage cheese, 1 egg, 1/2 cup sugar, lemon rind (to taste), and a pinch of salt. Place about 1 tablespoon of filling on each crepe. Spread and roll up like a jelly roll. Put them aside in a casserole dish.

Take 2 eggs, 2 cups milk, 1/2 cup sugar, pinch of salt and mix well like a custard. Pour over the crepes. Bake at 350 degrees for 1 hour.

I sometimes put a few chopped nuts in the filling.

Cherry Rolly Polly

Make sweet biscuit dough by sifting together 1½ cups flour, 2 teaspoons baking powder, ¼ teaspoon salt, ¼ teaspoon baking soda and 2 tablespoons sugar. Mix dry ingredients with ½ stick margarine until crumbly. Add ½ cup buttermilk. Mix well.

Roll this dough into a 12" x 9" rectangle. Spread with a little butter. Sprinkle with sugar and cinnamon. Drain a can of red cherries. Save juice. Place cherries evenly over dough. Roll up as for a jelly roll and cut into 1" slices. Put cut sides down on baking pan.

Take cherry juice and add ½ cup water, and ½ cup sugar and bring to a boil. Thicken with a teaspoon corn starch mixed with a little water. Take off stove. Add ½ teaspoon almond extract. Pour over cherry slices and bake at 350 degrees for 25-30 minutes.

This is good served with ice cream or whipped cream. This is one of my daugther Carol's favorites.

Pie Crust

This makes enough for 2 pie shells. You may ½ the recipe for single pie shell. Take ½ cup margarine, ¼ cup boiling water and a pinch of salt and beat with a wire whisk until it is the consistency of heavy cream. Add 2 cups flour. Mix with a fork until crumbly. If too soft add more flour. Divide dough in ½ to make 2 balls. Roll each out between 2 pieces of plastic wrap to make a round crust. Carefully place in pie plate. Trim edges and flute by pressing between your fingers. Use baked or unbaked as specified in recipe.

Shoo Fly Pie

Sift 1¼ cups flour, ½ cup sugar, ¼ teaspoon salt, ½ teaspoon nutmeg and 1 teaspoon cinnamon. Cut into this ½ cup margarine (with a knife or mix with your hands) until you have fine crumbs. Take 1 cup molasses, 1 cup cold water, ½ teaspoon baking soda and mix well. Pour into unbaked pie shell. Sprinkle crumbs on top. Bake for 15 minutes at 450 degrees, then 40 minutes at 350 degrees.

Butterscotch Pie

1 3/4 cups milk
1 cup brown sugar
2 eggs, separated
2 tablespoons flour
1 tablespoon corn starch
pinch salt
butter the size of a walnut
1 teaspoon vanilla

Put 1 1/2 cups milk in a pan and heat. Mix brown sugar, egg yolks, flour, corn starch and salt with 1/4 cup milk. Slowly pour hot milk over this mixture. Bring to a boil. Stir until thick. Add lump of butter and vanilla. Pour into a baked pie crust.

To make meringue: Beat 2 egg whites until stiff. Slowly add 4 tablespoons sugar. Spread meringue evenly over pie filling. Bake 10 to 15 minutes at 350 degrees until meringue is light brown.

Lemon Sponge Pie

2 eggs, separated
1 lemon
1 cup sugar
2 tablespoons flour
1 tablespoon butter
¼ teaspoon salt
1 cup milk

    Mix sugar, flour and egg yolks in a bowl. Mix in lemon juice squeezed from 1 lemon. Add soft butter and grated rind of the lemon. Add 1 cup milk. Mix well. Beat egg whites. Gently fold in the beaten egg whites. Pour into an unbaked pie crust. Bake at 350 degrees for 45 minutes to 1 hour.

    This is a very old recipe and has a most delicate flavor.

Apple Pie with Cheese Crumbs

Make the pie crust recipe and bake at 350 degrees for about 10 minutes so it is pale brown. Remove from oven and set aside.

For the crumbs: 1/2 cup flour, 1/2 cup sugar, 1/2 stick margarine, 1/4 cup grated sharp cheese. Mix together with your hands until crumbly.

Peel and core 6 apples. Slice them about 1/4" thick. Put in a sauce pan with 3/4 cup sugar, 1 tablespoon tapioca, a dash cinnamon, and mace, a sprinkle of lemon juice and 1/4 cup water. Bring to a boil and simmer for about 5 minutes. Pour into the pie shell. Sprinkle with crumbs and bake about 30 minutes in a 350 degree oven.

Dill Cheese Pie

¼ cup butter, 1 pound cottage cheese, 3 eggs separated, 1 tablespoon lemon juice, grated rind of 1 lemon, 3/4 cup sugar, ¼ teaspoon salt, 1 cup cream or evaporated milk, 2 tablespoons corn starch, 1 teaspoon vanilla, 1 tablespoon chopped fresh dill, 1 unbaked pie crust.

Beat butter and cottage cheese until smooth. Add lemon juice, lemon rind, sugar, salt and egg yolks. Mix well. Mix corn starch with cream and vanilla. Add this and the dill to the cottage cheese mixture. Beat egg whites and fold into the cheese mixture. Pour into pie crust and bake at 400 degrees for 10 minutes, then 350 degrees for 1 hour.

∽

This pie is one I usually bake in the summer when I can pick dill fresh from the garden. This is one of Carrie's favorites!

∽

You can also make this by leaving out the dill and pouring 1 can of drained, crushed pineapple in the pie crust before pouring the cheese mixture.

Cherry Custard Pie

Make the pie crust recipe and bake at 350 degrees for about 10 minutes so it is pale brown. Remove from oven and set aside.

Make custard with 1 3/4 cups milk, 1/2 cup sugar, pinch of salt, 2 eggs separated, 1 tablespoon corn starch and 2 tablespoons flour. Mix dry ingredients in a bowl. Add 2 egg yolks and 2-3 tablespoons milk. Stir until well blended. Bring the 1 3/4 cups milk to a boil. Pour <u>slowly</u> over the blended egg mixture. Put back on the stove and cook until thickened. Remove from heat. Add 1 teaspoon vanilla and 1 tablespoon butter. Blend. Pour into pie shell. Beat the 2 egg whites until stiff. Add 4 tablespoons of sugar slowly. When nice and stiff put meringue around the edges of the custard leaving the center open. Bake 10-15 minutes at 350 degrees until meringue is pale brown. When cool, fill center with red cherry pie filling.

This is a very old fashioned recipe.

Zinzer Torte

Take 1 3/4 cups flour, 1 teaspoon baking powder, 1/2 cup sugar, 1/4 teaspoon salt, 1/2 teaspoon cinnamon, 1/8 teaspoon cloves, 1 egg and 1 1/4 stick of margarine.

Mix dry ingredients together. Rub in the margarine with your hands. Add egg and form into a ball.* Take 1/2 of the dough and roll out to 1/8" thick. Put into an 8" x 10" pan. Take the rest of the dough and with your hands roll into pencil thin strips. Criss cross the strips over the dough in the pan to make a lattice work effect. Put a teaspoon of raspberry** jam into each section made by the strips. Bake 15 to 20 minutes at 350 degrees.

* If dough is tacky, add more flour to make it workable.

** Other jams may be substituted.

Oatmeal Cookies

1 cup white sugar
1 cup brown sugar
2 eggs
3 cups oatmeal
1 cup margarine
1 cup flour
1 teaspoon baking soda
½ cup chopped nuts
½ cup raisins
½ cup coconut

Cream sugar, margarine and eggs until light and fluffy. Add flour, oatmeal and baking soda. Add nuts, raisins and coconut. Mix well. Drop from a teaspoon on greased cookie sheet. Bake 10 to 12 minutes at 350 degrees.

Grandma's Sugar Cookies

1 cup margarine, 2 cups sugar, 2/3 teaspoon baking soda, 1/2 teaspoon salt, 1 teaspoon vanilla, 3 eggs (beaten), 3 2/3 cups flour, 2 teaspoons baking powder and sugar to sprinkle.

Cream margarine with sugar, baking soda and vanilla. Add eggs. Mix well. Add sifted flour, salt and baking powder. Chill. On a well floured surface roll 1/8" thick. Cut with cookie cutter and sprinkle with sugar. Bake at 350 until light brown - 8 to 10 minutes. Very old recipe.

Sand Tarts

Cream 1/2 cup margarine with 1 cup sugar and 1 egg. Add a pinch of mace or 1/2 teaspoon grated lemon rind. Sift 2 cups flour, 2 teaspoons baking powder and 1/4 teaspoon salt. Mix sifted ingredients in with creamed mixture. Shape into a ball and chill for 1/2 hour. On a well floured surface roll out to 1/8" thick. Brush with a beaten egg. Combine 1/4 cup sugar, 1/4 teaspoon cinnamon and 1/2 cup chopped nuts. Sprinkle this over the dough and roll with rolling pin. Cut in 1" x 3" strips. Bake at 350 degrees for 12 minutes or until golden brown.

Bohemian Nut Slices

Dissolve 1 package yeast and 1 teaspoon sugar in 1/4 cup warm water. Take 2 cups flour, 1/2 teaspoon salt, 3/4 cup margarine, 2 eggs (separated) 1/2 cup sugar, 1/4 cup nuts and 1 teaspoon vanilla.

Sift flour and salt. Cut in margarine. Add egg yolks and softened yeast. Mix into a ball. Beat egg whites until stiff. Gradually add sugar and vanilla. Fold in chopped nuts.

Take ball of dough and roll into a sheet about 9" x 13". Cut into 2 halves. Spread the nut filling over each piece leaving 1/2" edge without filling. Roll up like a jelly roll. Place each on a baking sheet. With a knife cut 1/2" slit down the center of the roll. Bake immediately, 25 minutes at 375 degrees. When it's done, while still warm, sprinkle with powdered sugar. Slice diagonally into 1/2" slices.

They look festive to serve with tea.

Polish Pretzels or Snow Balls

2 cups flour, 1 tablespoon sugar, 1/2 teaspoon salt, 3 egg yolks, 1/2 cup sour cream, 1 jigger of brandy and 1 teaspoon vanilla.

Sift flour, sugar and salt. Make a well in the center and add the egg yolks, sour cream and flavorings. Make dough so it can be well handled. Cut into 2 pieces. Roll each out about 1/8" thickness. Cut into 3" or 4" squares. Make 2 slits* in each square. Have a pan of hot oil ready. Take each square and pull the corners through the slits. Drop into the hot oil. Cook on both sides turning once. They should be golden brown. Drain on a paper towel. Sprinkle heavily with powdered sugar.

*

They are very festive looking and are nice for an afternoon tea or buffet luncheon.

Shortbread

½ cup butter, ⅔ cup powdered sugar, 1 teaspoon vanilla, 1 large egg yolk, 2 tablespoons
milk, 1½ cups flour, sifted, ¼ cup chopped
walnuts and ½ cup chopped coconut.

Combine all ingredients. Mix well. Roll into
2 balls and refrigerate for at least 2 hours.
Roll out ¼" thick in round shape. Mark 8 wedges
with a knife. It is nice to use a shortbread pan
but if you don't have one you can place the 2
rounds on a cookie sheet. Bake at 350 degrees
until pale tan, about 15-20 minutes. Be very
careful it doesn't get too dark.

Meringues

3 egg whites, 1 cup sugar, ½ teaspoon each of
vanilla and vinegar.

Beat egg whites until stiff. Add sugar slowly
while beating. Fold in vanilla and vinegar. Spoon
onto baking sheet. Make "peaks" the size of golf balls,
or 4" shells hollowed out with the back of spoon.
Bake at 300 degrees until pale, pale brown. Dry in

oven with heat turned off for ½ hour. The shells make a delicious dessert filled with vanilla ice cream topped with fresh strawberries or raspberries and topped with whipped cream. The "peaks" are delicious on their own as a light, melt-in-your-mouth treat!

Potato Doughnuts

2 cups flour, ½ teaspoon salt, 2 teaspoons baking powder, ¼ teaspoon nutmeg, 1 cup sugar, 1 cup riced or mashed potatoes, 1 tablespoon butter and 2 eggs. Mix all ingredients together. Make a soft dough. Roll out about ¼" thick. Cut with a doughnut cutter. Fry until golden brown in oil on medium heat. Drain on a paper towel. Sprinkle with powdered sugar.

Apple Squares

3 cups flour, 1½ teaspoons baking powder, 1½ cups sugar and 1 teaspoon salt. Sift all together. Then cut in 3/4 cup margarine (or mix in with your hands). Add 2 egg yolks and ¼ cup milk. Mix into a ball. Divide in ½. Roll out ½ of the dough to fit on a 9"x 15" cookie sheet. Roll out the other ½ for the top.

For the filling: Shred 2 or 3 apples. Add 1 cup raisins, 2 teaspoons cinnamon, 1 cup sugar and ¼ cup chopped nuts. Mix well. Beat the 2 egg whites and fold into the apple mixture. Place the filling on the dough and spread evenly. Cover with remaining ½ of dough. Brush with a little egg white remaining in bowl and sprinkle with sugar. Bake at 375 degrees for 20 to 30 minutes. When slightly cooled cut into 2" squares and sprinkle liberally with powdered sugar.

We all love these and they really look delicious!

95

Joan's Brownies

3/4 cup oil or margarine, 1 1/2 cups sugar, 3 eggs, 2 1/2 tablespoons cocoa, 1 cup flour, 1/2 teaspoon baking powder, pinch of salt, 1 teaspoon vanilla and 1/2 cup chopped nuts.

Cream the oil or margarine with sugar. Add eggs one at a time. Cream after each egg is added. Add vanilla. Add the dry sifted ingredients and nuts. Mix well. Spread in a well greased square pan. Bake at 350 degrees for 30 minutes. May be thinly iced if you prefer. Cut into small squares while warm.

For icing: Combine 1 generous tablespoon of margarine, 1 teaspoon cocoa (or 2 if you want it real chocolaty), 1 capful vanilla, 1/2 to 3/4 cup powdered sugar and 1 to 2 tablespoons milk. You can use more or less of the powdered sugar and milk depending on the amount of icing and consistency you want. It should be smooth and easy to spread.

These never fail, are most delicious and taste almost like fudge.

Basic Sweet Dough

Sift 6 to 7 cups flour with ½ cup sugar and 1 teaspoon salt. Take 2 packages of yeast and 1 teaspoon sugar and dissolve in ¼ cup warm water. Warm 1 cup milk, ½ cup water and ½ cup margarine. When margarine is melted add 2 beaten eggs. Make a well in flour mixture. Add milk mixture and yeast mixture. Mix well. Then knead it until soft and satiny. Use more flour if necessary. Place in a greased bowl and let rise until double in bulk. When it is risen you can take it out and knead some more on the table.

You can make a number of delicious and simple recipes from this dough. On the next pages I have written several things that can be made from this dough after it has risen.

Doughnuts

This dough may also be made into doughnuts. Roll out ¼" thick. Cut with a doughnut cutter. Let rise until double. Fry in oil on a medium heat. Coat with sugar when done.

Jelly Buns

Take ½ of the sweet dough recipe and roll out on a floured board to ¼" thick. Cut circles of dough with a cutter or glass about 3" round. Put a teaspoon of jam of your preference in the center. I like to use raspberry. Draw up the edges and pinch shut. Place side by side in a well buttered baking pan. Make crumbs with ½ cup sugar, ½ cup flour, and ¼ cup butter. Mix well. Sprinkle on top of the cakes. Let rise until double. Bake at 350 degrees for 20 to 30 minutes.

Cinnamon Buns

Take ½ of the dough. Roll it into a rectangle about ¼" thick. Spread melted butter over it. Then a thin layer of brown sugar, and sprinkle with cinnamon, raisins and nuts. Roll up like a jelly roll and cut into 1" thick slices. Into a well buttered pan sprinkle a thick layer of brown sugar, ¼ cup syrup or honey and 3 tablespoons water. Lay the slices (cut side up) side by side in the pan. Cover and let rise until double. Bake at 375 degrees for 20 to 30 minutes. Take out of the pan while still hot.

Pull Apart Cake

Take ½ of the dough and pull off pieces the size of a walnut. Roll in your hands to make a ball. Dip into melted butter. Dip into a mixture of ½ cup brown or white sugar, ½ cup nuts and ½ teaspoon cinnamon. Cover each piece well with nut mixture then drop into a well buttered spring mold. When half full, let rise until double. Bake at 350 degrees for 30 minutes. This is a great favorite. When serving just pull the pieces off the cake.

Apple Cakes

Take ½ of the sweet dough after it has risen. Roll out on a floured board to about ¼" thick. Cut the dough into 3" squares. Pare 2 apples and cut into ¼" thick slices crosswise (so you have round slices). Remove cores. Place apple slices in center of dough squares. Put a bit of butter, a teaspoon sugar and sprinkle of cinnamon on each apple slice. Draw corners of the square over top of the apple slice and press together. Place into a well buttered pan. Brush with melted butter and sprinkle with sugar. Let rise until double. Bake at 325 degrees for 20 to 30 minutes. Should be golden. Most delicious!

Butter Cake

Take about 1/3 of the dough and roll it out 1/4" thick. Put in a well buttered pan. (9"x 12" or 10"x 14') For topping use 1/4 pound butter, 1 cup sugar, 1/3 cup flour, 1 large egg and 3 tablespoons milk. Beat with a mixer until light and fluffy. Spread evenly on top of the dough. Let rise until double. Bake at 375 degrees for 30 minutes.

Prune Dumplings
or Dampf Noodles

Take 1/2 of the dough. Roll out 1/2" thick. Cut into 3" circles. Cook 1/2 pound prunes with 2 teaspoons sugar and water until tender. Cool. Grease a deep fryingpan or dutch oven well. Sprinkle with 3/4 cup brown sugar and lay the circles in the pan. Let rise until double. Place the cooked prunes around them and pour the prune juice over them. Cook very slowly. Cover for 15 minutes. Remove lid and turn them over. Cover and cook 10 minutes until done. Heat must be low as they burn easily. Put on a serving platter and pour the syrup over them. Very sweet and most delicious!

Ring-a-lings

⅓ cup butter, ⅓ cup sugar, 2 packages yeast, ¼ cup warm water, ¾ cup hot milk, ½ teaspoon salt, 2 teaspoons orange rind, 2 eggs, 4-5 cups flour.

<u>For Filling</u>: Cream ⅓ cup butter. Blend in 1 cup powdered sugar and 1 cup chopped nuts.
<u>For Glaze</u>: Mix ¼ cup orange juice with 3 tablespoons sugar.

Blend butter and sugar. Add orange rind, eggs and salt. Dissolve yeast in warm water. Add and mix with butter mixture. Add hot milk. Add sifted flour. Dough must be so you can roll it out. Let rise. Roll into a 10"x12" rectangle. Spread with nut filling. Fold in half so now you have a 5"x 12" rectangle. Cut 1" strips so you have 12- 5"x1" strips. Twist each one. Wrap around and tuck the end under so now you have a circle. Let rise. Bake at 350 degrees for 15 minutes until golden brown. Spread with glaze. Bake 5 minutes more. *We really love these!*

1"x 5"   TWisted   circle

Lazy Time Sponge Cake

1 cup scalded milk
1/4 cup butter
4 eggs
1 3/4 cups sugar
1 teaspoon vanilla
1 3/4 cups flour
1 tablespoon baking powder
1/2 teaspoon salt

Scald milk in a saucepan. Add butter and melt. Separate eggs. Whip whites with 1/2 cup sugar. Put the rest of the sugar into a mixing bowl. Add egg yolks and vanilla. Cream until light and fluffy. Add sifted flour, baking powder and salt. Add vanilla and scalded milk. Mix well. Gently fold in the egg whites. Pour into a spring mold or a 9" x 13" baking pan. Bake at 350 degrees for 35 minutes.

This cake is delicious plain or made into strawberry or peach shortcake. With the shortcake I use whipped cream on top. On the next page is a special way I prepare this cake which my family all love.

Special Chocolate Cake

Take 1½ cups sugar, 3 tablespoons cocoa, pinch salt and ½ cup milk and cook over a slow heat. Cook until done. It is done when you test it by placing a drop of the mixture in cold water and the mixture stays together in a ball. Pour mixture over a beaten egg. Add 1 teaspoon vanilla and butter the size of a walnut. When this is well mixed pour it over a beaten egg white. Beat until ready to spread, not letting it get too thick.

In the meantime have the Lazy Time Sponge Cake ready. I use a 9"x 13" pan. When cool cut in ½ then cut each ½ through the middle making 4 layers. Put this all together by frosting each side and layering one on top of the other. The frosting will be thin, but it hardens. When ready to serve spread with whipped cream on top. Garnish with maraschino cherries.

Very festive and delicious!

Sunburst Chiffon Cake

In a bowl mix 1 cup flour, 3/4 cup sugar, 1 1/2 teaspoons baking powder and 1/2 teaspoon salt. Make a well and add 1/4 cup salad oil, 3 egg yolks, 3/8 cup cold water (1/4 cup and 2 tablespoons) and the grated rind of 1 orange. Beat until smooth. In a bowl put 4 egg whites and 1/4 teaspoon cream of tartar. Beat until very stiff. Fold into flour mixture. Bake at 350 degrees for 30 to 35 minutes. Bake in a spring mold or a flat pan.

You can make a delicious Boston Cream Pie with this. Just cut in 1/2 when it's done and fill with either lemon or vanilla pudding. Then ice the top with chocolate frosting.

You can have a delicious strawberry shortcake too. Cut in 1/2 and fill with whipped cream mixed with sliced strawberries. Top with whipped cream and garnish with whole strawberries.

This is a very tender textured cake.

Best Pound Cake

I have been making this cake for years and it is one of the easiest and one of the best. For best results use sweet butter. It is alright to use margarine.

Take 2/3 cup butter and 1¼ cups sugar and cream well. Add ½ teaspoon lemon rind, 1 teaspoon vanilla, pinch of mace or nutmeg and 1 jigger of rum. Sift 2 cups flour, ½ teaspoon salt and ½ teaspoon baking powder. Blend with butter and sugar mixture with 2/3 cup milk. When blended add 3 eggs, one at a time beating each one in well. If preferred add ½ cup nuts or currants. Pour into a loaf pan or a spring mold. Bake at 325 degrees for 1 hour and 15 minutes.

Sour Cream Pound Cake

1 cup butter, 3 cups sugar, 1 teaspoon vanilla, 6 large eggs, 3 cups flour, 1/4 teaspoon baking soda, 1/8 teaspoon salt, 8 ounces sour cream.

Cream butter and sugar. Add vanilla. Add eggs one at a time. Beat well after each egg is added. Add sour cream. Sift flour, baking soda and salt. Add flour mixture. Mix well. Pour mixture into a buttered and floured Bundt pan. Bake for 1 hour at 350 degrees. Cool on wire rack.

It is better to use a Bundt pan when baking pound cakes because it bakes faster. If you use the "traditional" bread pan it takes longer and therefore becomes dry.

Chocolate Sour Cream Pound Cake

1 cup butter, 2 cups sugar, 1 cup brown sugar, 2 teaspoons vanilla, 6 large eggs, 2 1/2 cups flour, 1/4 teaspoon baking soda, 1/8 teaspoon salt, 1/2 cup cocoa, 8 ounces sour cream. Same directions as above. Sift cocoa with other dry ingredients.

Jelly Roll

4 eggs, 3/4 cup flour, sifted, 1 teaspoon baking powder, 1/4 teaspoon salt, 3/4 cup sugar, 1 teaspoon vanilla, powdered sugar, 1 cup current or strawberry jam.

Mix eggs at high speed until thick. Gradually beat in sugar. Add vanilla. Sift flour, baking powder and salt. Blend in dry ingredients. Grease and flour a 10" x 15" baking pan. Pour batter into pan and bake at 350 degrees for 10-13 minutes. When done loosen edges with a knife and invert on a towel sprinkled with powdered sugar. Immediately roll up with towel. This keeps the cake from sticking. Let cake cool like this. When cool, unroll and spread with jam. Roll back up and sprinkle with powdered sugar through a sifter.

You can use other fillings like pudding or fresh whipped cream plain or mix with fresh fruit such as strawberries. This is a very pretty, elegant dessert!

Devil's Food Cake

Take ½ cup sugar, 3/4 cup cocoa and ¼ cup water and bring to a boil over a low fire. Cool slightly.

Take 1 cup sugar, 2 eggs, ½ cup margarine, 1 teaspoon vanilla and cream well. Sift 2 cups flour, 1 teaspoon baking soda and ¼ teaspoon salt. Add and blend with the creamed mixture. Add 2/3 cup buttermilk. Blend in the cocoa mixture. Lastly, add ½ cup boiling water. Pour into 2 buttered layer pans and bake at 350 degrees for 30 minutes.

This makes a most delicious fudgy cake. I use it with chocolate frosting. It can also be filled and spread with whipped cream.

A Delicious Applesauce Cake

   1 cup margarine, 2 cups sugar, 2 eggs, 2½ cups flour, 1½ teaspoons baking soda, 1 teaspoon cinnamon, ½ teaspoon nutmeg, ¼ teaspoon cloves, 1½ cups applesauce, ½ cup chopped nuts and ½ cup raisins. Cream butter, sugar and eggs. Add flour, baking soda and spices with the nuts and raisins. Add applesauce. Mix well. Bake at 350 degrees for 45 minutes.

Kathie's Ginger Cake

   4 cups flour, 1 cup sugar, 1 cup brown sugar, ½ pound margarine, 1 cup molasses, 2 cups boiling water and 1 teaspoon baking soda. Mix the first 4 ingredients until crumbly. Keep 1½ cups for crumbs for on top of cake. To the remaining crumbs add molasses mixed with boiling water. Mix well. Pour into an 8"x 10" pan. Sprinkle the top with crumbs. Bake at 325 degrees for 1 hour.

   This makes a most delicious moist cake. Inexpensive too!

Jetta's Coffee Cake

Dissolve 1 package of yeast in 1/4 cup warm water. 3 eggs (separated), 1/2 cup milk, 3 1/4 cups flour, 1 1/4 cups sugar, 1 teaspoon salt, 1 cup margarine, 1 1/2 teaspoons lemon rind, 1 cup nuts and powdered sugar.

Beat egg yolks. Beat in milk and yeast. In a large bowl combine 3 cups flour, 1/4 cup sugar and salt. Cut in butter. Stir in yeast mixture and lemon rind. Let stand for 30 minutes. Stir in 1/4 cup flour. Knead until smooth and satiny. Put into greased bowl. Grease the top, cover and refrigerate overnight. Let stand at room temperature for a few minutes. Press with your hands to soften and warm. Roll to a 12"x 16" rectangle.

To make filling: Stir together egg whites, nuts and 1 cup sugar. Spread over dough. Roll up like a jelly roll. Put into greased bundt pan. Let rise 2 to 2 1/2 hours. Bake at 325 degrees for 1 hour and 15 minutes. Cool in the pan for 15 minutes. Put on a plate and sprinkle with powdered sugar. Delicious!

Poppyseed Cake

1 can poppyseed filling, 1 cup margarine, 1½ cup sugar, 4 eggs separated, 1 teaspoon vanilla, 1 cup sour cream, 2½ cup flour, 1 teaspoon baking soda and ½ teaspoon salt.

Cream margarine, sugar and egg yolks until fluffy. Add the poppyseed filling. Sift dry ingredients. Add sour cream. Add dry ingredients. Beat egg whites until stiff and _fold_ into the mixture. Pour into greased bundt pan and bake at 350 degrees for about 1 hour. Test with toothpick or straw. The cake is done when it comes out clean. When cool, sprinkle with powdered sugar or serve with whipped cream.

Coconut Vanities

1½ cups flour, 1½ teaspoons baking powder, 4 tablespoons butter, 1 cup sugar, 1 egg, rind of 1 orange, ¼ cup milk, ½ cup orange juice and coconut flakes.

Cream sugar, butter, egg and orange rind. Sift flour and baking powder. Add flour mixture to creamed mixture and blend. Add milk and orange juice. Mix well. Spread dough on a cookie sheet. Make a meringue with 1 beaten egg white and 4 tablespoons sugar. Spread meringue evenly over dough. Sprinkle with coconut flakes. Bake at 350 degrees for 20 minutes. Cool. Slice diagonally to make diamond shaped cakes.

This is a very old fashioned recipe. It's very festive and inexpensive too. I made it many times during the depression for my children. I especially remember serving these cakes on Saturday nights when my brother, Nick, and his wife would come over to play cards. They were hard times, but we enjoyed the simple pleasures throughout the depression.

Christmas Specialties

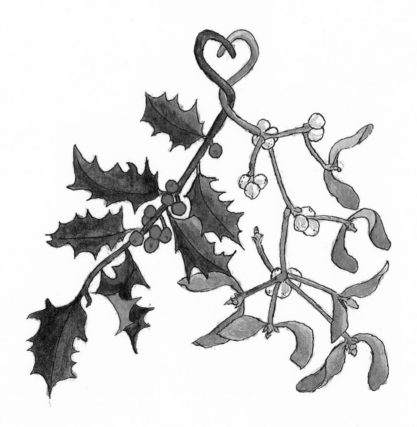

Mistletoe and Holly

Mistletoe and Holly - the signs of Christmas. This time of year is so special. There is something mystic in the air. Everyone seems to be filled with a feeling of expectation. The feelings of love and joy surround you. You think of your loved ones and want to be with them. People smile at you and you feel it too. Not only at Christmas but somehow the whole year through, the joy that you give to others is the joy that comes back to you!

Christmas Remembered...
9 years old

Christmas when I was a little girl was so different than it is now. Not having radio or television everything was pictured in my imagination, which was very vivid. It starts with the last day of school. I went to a one room little stone school house with 8 grades and one teacher. We had our Christmas program in the afternoon. Then wonder of wonders, we heard sleigh bells and Santa Claus suddenly came bounding through the door with his big pack! He presented each child with a ½ lb. of chocolates which I took home to my brothers with much pride.

When mother put us to bed that night we were so full of delicious anticipation of what tomorrow would bring that it took us a long time to fall asleep. At this time I had three brothers. We all slept in a room above the kitchen, as we had no central heat and it was warm there.

In the morning we crept down the stairs and there was the Christmas tree - so beautiful in our eyes. It was a cedar tree that mother had cut down

from the woods. It had a silver steeple on top and I particularly remember a beautiful red and gold slipper and a sail boat all covered with gold wire. All of the lit small candles in their holders made it look magical! Beside the tree was a sled, our first "American Flyer". We had so much fun with it that winter. It seemed we had much more snow in those years. Then there were all of the special goodies under the tree - oranges, nuts, dates, figs, candy - all special at Christmastime. Before we went to bed that night, mother would light all of the little candles on the tree. We would stand before it and in German sing "Silent night". My father had a wonderful tenor voice and the feeling of reverence for this special day stayed with me always. Until this day when I smell candle wax I am transported to those childhood Christmas' and the feeling of mystery and expectation we all had.

"Stille nacht, Heilige nacht."..

Nut and Poppyseed Roll

Traditionally I always make this bread for Christmas. My husband and I trimmed the tree on Christmas Eve. After our work was done, we would sit next to it with all of our anticipated excitment and enjoy a slice of bread and a cup of coffee. On Christmas morning our children would open their presents and gaze up at the tree in all it's glory. Then we would always have the nut and poppyseed roll with butter for a special Christmas breakfast.

Take 1 cup scalded milk, 1 cup sour cream, ½ cup sugar, ½ cup melted margarine, 1 teaspoon salt, 2 packages yeast dissolved in ½ cup warm water and 2 beaten eggs. Mix all ingredients together. Add about 6 cups flour. Mix well. Cover and let stand in the refrigerator overnight. The next day divide into 2 portions. Knead each piece well. Roll each piece into a 9" x 15" sheet. Spread with filling and roll up like a jelly roll. Filling recipes on the next page. Place on a well greased cookie sheet. Brush the top with a beaten egg yolk (mix with a little milk) Sprinkle with sugar. Let rise in a warm place until double. Bake at 350 degrees for 30 to 40 minutes.

Nut Filling

Take 1 cup ground nuts, 1/2 cup sugar, 1/2 cup milk and 1/2 cup chopped dates. Put into a saucepan and cook over a low heat until thick. Cool. Fold in 1 whipped egg white.

⤿

Poppyseed Filling

For the poppyseed roll I use a jar of poppyseed filling. Sprinkle with raisins and nuts.

⤿

You may add raisins and citron to the nut roll if desired.

⤿

Cinnamon Stars

In a small mixing bowl beat 3 egg whites until soft peaks form. Increase to a higher speed and add 2 cups powdered sugar a little at a time until stiff and glossy. Set aside 1 cup of this mixture. Beat 2 teaspoons grated lemon rind, 1 tablespoon ground cinnamon and 1/8 teaspoon salt into remaining meringue mixture. Fold in 8 ounces of ground almonds or walnuts.

Lightly flour work surface. Sprinkle with granulated sugar. Turn meringue with nuts onto the work surface and spread out about 3/8" thick. Let stand uncovered for 30 minutes. Using floured rolling pin, roll out dough 1/4" thick. Cut out with floured star shaped cookie cutter. Re-flour each time. Arrange on cookie sheet. With back of spoon spread the top of each cookie with a small amount of reserved meringue mixture. Bake at 275 degrees for 14 to 16 minutes. Cool on rack. Store in an air tight tin.

Christmas Kiffle

Take 4 cups flour, 1 tablespoon baking powder, ½ teaspoon salt, ½ cup sweet butter, and ½ cup margarine. Mix these ingredients into fine crumbs.

Dissolve 1 package yeast in ¼ cup warm water. Add to first mixture with 4 egg yolks and 1 cup sour cream. Shape into a ball and refrigerate overnight. The next day take ¼ of the dough and roll out ⅛" thick. Cut into squares about 3"x 3". Put ½ teaspoon filling in the center of each square. Starting at 1 corner, roll it up and shape into a crescent. Bake at 350 degrees for 15 to 20 minutes. Sprinkle with powdered sugar.

For Filling: 1 cup chopped nuts, ½ cup chopped dates, ½ cup sugar, ¼ cup water. Cook the dates, sugar and water about 10 minutes until thick. Add the nuts. Cool. Fold in 1 beaten egg white. You can use jam instead of this filling.

Christmas Butter Cookies

Cream ½ pound butter, 2 eggs, 1⅓ cups sugar, 4 tablespoons milk, 1 teaspoon vanilla and the rind of ½ a lemon. Sift 3⅔ cups flour, ¼ teaspoon salt and 2½ teaspoons baking powder.* Add to creamed mixture. Mix well. Chill dough for at least 2 hours. That way it is much easier to handle. Roll out very thin. Cut with desired cookie cutters. Brush with a mixture of 1 egg yolk and 1 tablespoon milk. Sprinkle with jimmies, sugar or nuts. I like to make a meringue with 1 beaten egg white and 2 tablespoons sugar. Place a ½ teaspoonful on the center of each cookie and sprinkle with nuts and sugar. Bake at 350 degrees for 10 to 12 minutes. Delicious!

Very delicate, crisp and festive!

* I sometimes add ⅛ teaspoon of mace which adds a special delicate flavor.

Crackled Ginger Snaps

3/4 cup margarine, 1½ cups sugar, 3 eggs, 4 teaspoons baking soda, 4 cups flour, 3/4 cup molasses, 1 teaspoon each of cinnamon and ginger.

Dissolve baking soda in 4 teaspoons of hot water. Cream oil, sugar and eggs. Add dissolved baking soda and molasses. Mix well. Sift flour and spices in. Mix well. Chill dough overnight in freezer. Roll out to about 1/8" thick. This is a very soft dough so you'll need to be generous with flour when rolling out. Cut with cookie cutters. Bake at 350 degrees for 10-12 minutes. When cool, decorate with frosting and jimmies. These keep very well.

These cookies are very crisp, and colorful when decorated!

French Love Cakes

½ pound margarine, 4 tablespoons sugar, 2 cups flour, pinch of salt, ½ teaspoon vanilla and 1 cup chopped pecans. Mix all together with your hands. Take pieces of dough the size of a walnut. Make into a _ball and flatten_ with _a glass_ or shape into _crescents_. Bake in a slow oven at _300 degrees_ for about _½ an hour until pale golden_. Remove from pan. Immediately sprinkle heavily with powdered sugar. They are very short and most delicious!

Springerle

4 eggs, 2 cups sugar, 1 teaspoon anise extract, 4 cups flour, 3/4 teaspoon baking soda, 2 tablespoons oil, anise seeds.

Blend eggs, sugar, oil and anise extract. Sift flour and baking soda together. Add to egg mixture and blend together. Roll out 1/2" thick on floured surface. Press on design or use a Springerle rolling pin. Cut out individual cookies and place on a lightly floured surface. Cover with a towel and let stand overnight. (Do not refrigerate) This is to let them dry and to "set" the design. Sprinkle a greased cookie sheet with anise seeds. Moisten the bottom of each cookie with water on your fingertip. Place on cookie sheet. Bake at 300 degrees for about 15 minutes.

Lebkuchen

1 cup chopped nuts, 1/4 cup chopped citron, 1/2 teaspoon grated lemon peel, 1/4 cup lemon juice, 3/4 cup honey, 1 1/4 cups granulated sugar, 1 1/2 tablespoons brandy, 3 3/4 cups flour, dash of salt, 1 teaspoon baking soda, 1/2 teaspoon cinnamon, dash of cloves and nutmeg. For garnish: green citron and candied cherries cut in half.

Glaze: 2 cups powdered sugar mixed with 1/3 cup water.

Heat sugar and honey over medium heat in a saucepan. Take off heat. Add lemon juice and lemon peel. Mix well. Let cool for 10 minutes. Add citron, nuts and brandy. Mix with a wooden spoon until blended. Sift flour, salt, baking soda and spices into a large bowl. Make a well in the center. Pour in honey mixture. Mix with spoon, then with your hands. Dough will be stiff. Chill for 1 hour. Roll out 1/4" thick. Cut with heart shaped cookie cutter. Place on a lightly greased cookie sheet. Decorate with garnish to make a flower. Bake 8-10 minutes until light brown. Brush with glaze while warm.

~Notes~

helpful hint:

Always add the flavorings (vanilla, almond
extract, lemon rind, etc.) with the creamed
butter mixture. Butter absorbs them more than
any other ingredient. The results are more
flavorful cakes and cookies!

~ Notes ~

helpful hint:

If you don't have buttermilk, use regular milk and add 2 teaspoons of vinegar to every cup.

~Notes~

helpful hint *

Egg whites beat up much fuller if they are at room temperature.

Delightful, Charming & Highly Recommended...

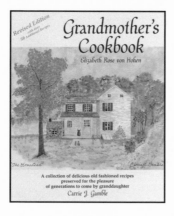

Revised Edition
with over 50 Additional Recipes

"It is a warm and loving book, one you would want to pass down to a new generation starting fresh. It sings with the traditions and heart of a real home. The recipes are easy and easy to like."

The Princeton Packet

"Highly recommended. A charming collection of memories, recipes & feelings from the heart."

Great Cookbooks Catalog
Simmer Pot Press

"If you often wish you'd thought of asking your grandmother to write down her favorite recipes, take heart. Carrie Gamble did."

New York Daily News

"The Perfect Gift"

Give Grandmother's Cookbook to Someone Special ...

The Bride-To-Be • Birthdays • Mother's Day • Christmas

Friends from afar • Friends moving afar • Her Hope Chest

Host/Hostess • House Warming • A Special "Thank You"

- -

To Order Grandmother's Cookbook
Revised Edition

You may contact your local bookstore or use the order form below.

I would like to order _____ cookbook(s) at $16.95 plus $3.00 shipping and handling for each copy (PA residents add $1.00 sales tax per copy).

☐ Autographed book(s) requested.   Amount Enclosed $ _____

NAME _____

ADDRESS _____

CITY _____ STATE _____ ZIP _____

PHONE (_____) _____

Send orders and make check payable to: **CARRIE J. GAMBLE, INC.**